PREACHING THE EASTER STORY

Hugh Litchfield

BROADMAN PRESS
Nashville, Tennessee

© Copyright 1987 • Broadman Press

4221-17

ISBN: 0-8054-2117-3

Dewey Decimal Classification: 232.97

Subject Heading: JESUS CHRIST - RESURRECTION // EASTER

Library of Congress Catalog Card Number: 86-14703

Printed in the United States of America

Unless otherwise indicated, Scripture quotations are from the Revised Standard Version of the Bible, copyrighted 1946, 1952, © 1971, 1973.

Scripture quotations marked (KJV) are from the King James Version of the Bible.

Library of Congress Cataloging-in-Publication Data

Litchfield, Hugh, 1940-
Preaching the Easter story.

  1. Easter—Sermons. 2. Holy-Week sermons.
3. Baptists—Sermons. 4. Sermons, American. I. Title.
BV4259.L57 1987 252'.63   86-14703
ISBN 0-8054-2117-3

To my mother and father
who were my teachers

To my children, Chris, Lynn, and Tim
who are my hope-givers

Preface

Easter is an exciting time to preach the good news of Christ. How wonderful to remember that God loves us so much that He was willing to send Christ to show us His love; He loves so much that He was willing to allow Christ to be crucified. But He knew something tremendous: Christ would overcome crucifixion and rise from the dead. "Christ is alive!" is the affirmation of our faith. That truth brings us hope in our battle against sin, encouragement in our struggle with suffering, and faith in the ultimate victory of life over death.

What I have presented in this book is a celebration of the amazing story of the resurrection of Christ. This event brings us face-to-face with the major issues and questions of life. The meaning of the events of that Passion Week continue to speak to us nearly two thousand years later. It is a word worth hearing over and over. I hope that what I have presented here will be of some help in understanding and proclaiming this truth.

I want to express my appreciation to the special people who are the Azalea Baptist Church of Norfolk, Virginia. Their encouragement and love and faith help me keep the resurrection truth alive in my life.

I would also like to thank the staff of Azalea for their encouragement and help as we seek to serve Christ together. The Reverend Jan Oberdick, Dr. Harold Hawn, and Mr. Bob Dailey are important people in my life, and I am thankful for the privilege to serve Christ with them.

Finally, I want to thank Mrs. Muriel Hoggard, the church secretary, for her faithfulness in typing the manuscript of this book. I appreciate her faithfulness, her patience, and her commitment to the task. Without her, these words would have been a long time coming.

Contents

Introduction

The heart of the Christian faith is the event of the resurrection. It is that which makes sense out of it all. As Paul wrote in his letter to the Corinthians, "But if there is no resurrection of the dead, then Christ has not been raised; if Christ has not been raised, then our preaching is in vain and your faith is in vain" (1 Cor. 15:13-14). The resurrection convinced them that sin could be defeated, that suffering could be overcome, and that death had no final power over them. The resurrection convinced them that Christ was truly the Son of God, worthy of worship and obedience. The resurrection is the heart of our faith.

Somehow people sense that. That is one reason churches are full on Easter Sunday. However faint the hope may be, many still cling to the truth that there is more to life than just what they experience on this earth, that there must be more beyond. So they come to church once again to hear that truth proclaimed, once again to renew the hope that can often get drowned in the sea of concerns this world presents. They come to hear again that life does not end in crucifixions but in resurrections.

One of the joyful tasks of a minister is to preach the truth of the resurrection. To have that good news to give is a tremendous privilege. But it is also an awesome responsibility. How can we present that truth in a way which will renew the hope of it? How can we make that truth take life so that it will reach out and stir the hearts and minds of the people? That is the challenge which faces the preacher as he stands to say, "He is risen; He is risen indeed!"

The old adage says, "Familiarity breeds contempt." This could be the danger of preaching on the resurrection. Since we ministers are always handling the dynamite of the truth of God, the fear is that the power of it may dwindle for us. We can get so used to preaching the resurrection that we no longer feel its excitement and joy. The overwhelming and amazing truth of the resurrection may seem like "old hat" to us. That must not happen.

In my own experience, I have found that the resurrection story really lives for me when I remember that it is not only about the heart of the faith but also about the basic issues of human life. In the events of Passion Week, the major conflicts of life are faced and conquered. To keep these important themes in mind can help us remember how important preaching the resurrection can be.

Resurrection Week Themes

Life Versus Death

Life versus death is one of the obvious themes of the crucifixion/ resurrection narratives. We live until we die, and death often seems like such an unwelcome visitor. It seems to be the final door that shuts tightly and cuts us off from all that we think is worthwhile. We talk a lot about living, but we don't like to talk about death. One preacher did a series on "Coming to Terms with Death." One of his members said, "I'm not going. I don't want to hear that morbid stuff." Most don't like to hear about it, but it is a part of life; we never really learn to live until we come to terms with what we think about death.

Easter gives us the opportunity to deal with the problem of death directly. Easter is the crucifixion with it's death and the resurrection with it's life. Which one is the word about us? Death cannot be avoided. Even Jesus had to face it, but it *can* be overcome. The resurrection is our assurance that death does not have the final say about our lives. Christ has conquered it. Death is only a door that leads to the resurrection and more beyond. Therefore, we do not need to go through life with a dread of death. In a sense, we can offer the laughter of faith in the face of it. It has no final power over us. That is a word that this world needs to hear.

Hope Versus Hopelessness

This is another vital theme of life. Hopelessness is no stranger to modern life. As we look around the world, it seems that crucifixions are the order of the day. All the wars, crime, hunger, poverty, prejudice, and so much more seem to wipe out the hope we have of a better world and of better things to come. Unfortunately, too many people do die of leukemia and cancer and heart disease. Unfortunately, too many people are lonely and feel left out of love and joy. As one young high school student said to me, "I don't see anything good to look forward to."

It is easy to give up hope. Then Christ rose from the dead! The message of the Christian faith is that hope is not in vain. There are crucifixions in the world, but they will be overcome by resurrections. It is not useless to look forward with hope because one day the kingdom of God Christ brought to earth through His presence will come in its fullness. The resurrection is God's promise that He will not disappoint us, that hope is not in vain, that the last word on life will not be a cross but an empty tomb. In the midst of hopelessness, we can live with hope because God will not let us down. That is a word worth hearing.

Suffering Versus Healing

Another one of the difficult questions of life centers around the terrible suffering that many have to face. Physical pain as well as mental pain is too much a part of life. "Why do people suffer?" That cry has been heard almost since the beginning of time. No easy answers can be given.

The cross brings us face-to-face with the issue of suffering. After all, Jesus was innocent, the best man who ever lived, and He was put on a cross to die. He suffered physical pain on the cross. Nails were driven through His hands and feet, a crown of thorns was put on His head, and a spear was thrust into His side. He suffered mentally also. He was ridiculed by others, forsaken by those He loved so dearly, and He even felt the inner anguish of the absence of God for a moment as He cried out, "My God, my God, why hast thou forsaken me?" (Mark 15:34). Christ knows what suffering is about because He went through it. We can know this: Christ is sympathetic to those who suffer. He knows what we are facing.

Then Christ rose from the dead! He overcame that suffering. That suffering, as terrible as it was, did not have the power to triumph over Christ. He knows how to defeat it. This is the word the resurrection message gives to the problem of suffering. It does not answer *why* we suffer, but it does tell us *how* we can handle suffering: with Christ's help and only with His help. Christ, who knew how to bear suffering and triumph over it, will help us face it. The Easter message is a word the sufferers need to hear.

Sin Versus Forgiveness

The power of sin is a reality of life. We struggle with sin constantly. It often seems to defeat us. We try to overcome it, but it's power seems too strong. We fight against alcoholism, gluttony, sexual maladjustments, injustices, or gossip; but we never seem to gain any mastery over them. Just like that Friday when Christ was nailed to the cross, sin seems to win the day. Christ came to fight against sin, but look where His fight got Him. On the cross, all the evil in the world was thrown at Him; and evil seemed to win. Christ suffered and died. Sin had won the day. It was too powerful, even for the Son of God.

But we must not stop with Friday. Too many people do. Too many people live as if Christ's death were the end. We must not forget that three days later Christ rose from the dead and that the death knell for sin was rung. Christ had said that He had the power to forgive sin, and the resurrection proved it. Sin was and is powerful, but it is not stronger than the power of God. He can not only help us fight sin but also give us forgiveness for it. Everyone needs to hear that word of hope. "All have sinned and fall short of the glory of God" (Rom. 3:23). But we do not have to be cut off forever from the glory of God. He can forgive us of our sin and give us a new chance to be His children. The power of sin does not have to triumph over us. Instead, the forgiveness of God can keep us going forward toward His kingdom. The resurrection affirms that Christ defeated the power of sin.

Hate Versus Love

The world is filled with hate, and love seems powerless in the face of it. As Christians, we are commanded to love everyone, even our enemies. Maybe we try to practice that, but when we do, our love often gets crucified. Love is often rejected, often ignored, often abused. The cross seems to be a good picture of what happens when we try to love. In the presence of power, hate, and anger, love seems so weak. Hate and anger and power crucified the love of God.

That was the way it seemed, but it was not the way it was. The love of Christ triumphed over the hate that put Him on the cross. His rising from the dead testified to the fact that the power of God's love is stronger than any power one can imagine. People could reject that love, mistreat that love, they could take it and crucify it, but it would keep on coming. Love would not be killed. It would not die. One can't destroy real love with guns or words or acts of hatred. God's love will still keep coming back, strong as ever.

Love may seem to be weak, especially when we try to give it. That is why we need the resurrection message. It encourages us to keep loving, to trust in it, and to live it. In the end, love will be successful. Love *is* eternal.

True Joy Versus False Joy

Those who crucified Christ were happy at His death. He was out of the way, and their way was seemingly proved right. They put their joy in the acquisition of material goods, and Christ challenged that. They felt they were right and Christ was wrong. They put their hope for joy in giving themselves to the pleasures of the flesh. Christ told them that would not satisfy. But with His death, they were sure that He was wrong. They put their hope for the joy of life in power, but Christ tried to point them to love. They were sure that they were right. Power crucified Christ. They counted on joy to be found in keeping the traditions of rituals and laws of their faith, but Christ tried to point them to service and concern for the hurting and the helpless. So they crucified Him because they did not think He was right. And they were full of joy.

Until the resurrection! Christ's resurrection seconded the motion to all that He had been teaching. Joy is not found in the temporary things of life but in one's relationship to God and others. True joy is found in the confidence that God will provide for our needs for all time. True joy is found in the understanding that nothing can ever separate us from the love of God. Jesus was right. Joy is not found in material things, earthly pleasures, human power, or even in keeping the traditions of the church. True joy is found in the peace and love and hope and faith that Christ brings to the heart. To love Christ and to serve others in His name is where joy is found. The shallow laughter of crucifixion Friday gives way to the true laughter of Easter morning.

Faith Versus Disbelief

The question of life may be what one feels is the final word about it: a crucifixion or a resurrection? Many do not believe the resurrection. They feel that life is summed up in that cross. Cruelty was there, and the cross stands as a symbol of man's inhumanity to man. Human beings hanged another person on a cross to die a slow and painful death. Others stood at the foot of the cross and laughed at the one being tortured and made fun of His being there. Such cruelty, such harshness, such indifference seemed to win out in the end. So many ask: How can one believe in the love and goodness of God when the best man who ever lived was treated like that? How can one believe in the goodness of humankind when that was allowed to happen? The conclusion is that there can be no God of love, no goodness inherent in people, no hope. The cross is how the world lives, and many choose to believe that the sooner one comes to terms with that, the better.

However, another option is available to all: the resurrection. The resurrection points to the power of God which can overcome evil and to the love of God which will make sure evil is overcome. God is working in life to bring about His kingdom. He can even take crosses and turn them into symbols not of death but of life. The world is not under the control of evil; it is under the control of God. Even though crucifixions occur far too often, faith holds onto God. God uses crosses to bring us life.

Modern humanity seems to be faced with a choice: Will we believe that the cross or the empty tomb was victorious? Can we trust God to help us overcome our cross experiences? The resurrection story presents that choice to everyone. The choice is either faith or disbelief, but the choice must be presented. Easter calls for a decision.

Defeat Versus Victory

The ultimate question presented by the resurrection event is: Was God defeated or did He triumph? On that Friday, it looked like He had been beaten. Sin and evil threw the worst at Jesus, and He died. On the cross, He was beaten. But we must not stop with the cross. The resurrection is the last word of God about how it all will end. The end time will come in a resurrection. It will end in the triumph of His ways. It will end in the establishment of the eternal kingdom of God, and all those who have trusted Him will share in that kingdom. Sin cannot stop the kingdom of God! Suffering cannot stop it! Even death cannot stop it! What God set out to do, He will do! When all is said and done, one kingdom will remain, and it will be the kingdom of God. Victory, not defeat, awaits those who are the children of God. No matter how many crucifixions we may face, the final experience for us will be resurrection. That is the joy and hope and promise of the gospel of Christ.

Preaching the Resurrection Story

We have a great message to preach during Passion Week. Palm Sunday, Maundy Thursday, Good Friday, and Easter cover the scope of the gospel and all the major events, moods, and major experiences of life. What a privilege to be able to preach it. I would like to offer a few practical suggestions.

Proclaim the Resurrection, Don't Debate It

One of the great temptations ministers can fall for is believing that we can argue people into believing the gospel. On Easter, the church is full with a lot of people who usually aren't there. This is the big chance to bring them into the fold by seeking to prove that the resurrection is a believable fact, even in this modern scientific age. So the arguments are brought in to persuade people to believe. Arguments from philosophy, illustrations from the world of nature, and practical reasons the resurrection makes sense—are paraded before the congregation with the belief that all who hear it will surely feel that the arguments are unquestionably right. Often people listen politely then leave quickly, never to be seen again until next Easter. I know this can happen because in the early years of my ministry I preached that way. I was always disappointed when the aisles did not fill with people who were persuaded that the resurrection was a truth of history.

I have learned that no matter how brilliant the arguments for the resurrection might be, one still can't prove it beyond the shadow of an intellectual doubt. Belief in the resurrection is a matter of faith, not a matter of intellectual assent. Very few people are argued into believing in Christ. It is not the great arguments of preachers but the Spirit of Christ which convicts people that Christ is risen from the dead and is alive.

What I feel we must do during the celebration of Passion Week is proclaim the gospel, not debate it. That is what the early disciples did. They went out to proclaim what had happened, to announce the event of the resurrection. Peter proclaimed on the day of Pentecost: "This Jesus, delivered up according to the definite plan and foreknowledge of God, you crucified and killed by the hands of lawless men. But God raised Him up, having loosed the pangs of death" (Acts 2:23-24). That is what we need to do on Easter Sunday. We need to announce what God has done, proclaim what the central beliefs of our faith are, and let the

Spirit of God apply them as He will. I suggest that we spend the precious moments of time we have to preach what we know is the heart of our faith. Christ is alive! That is what people need to hear. Whether they choose to believe it or not, they need to hear that truth proclaimed.

Be Positive and Not Negative

Another temptation that awaits the preacher on an Easter morning is to really "give it" to those persons who don't come to church, except on Easter or Christmas. Sometimes, church members expect the preacher to do that, to scold those who don't take the faith "seriously enough." So Easter sermons can turn into tirades against those who don't come like they should. The guilt is laid on thick and the fear of judgment preached with strong emphasis.

I have tried that way also, without much success. A few responded to such appeals and came to church more regularly for a while, but soon they drifted away again. Unless I kept up the guilt and the judgment, they did not respond all that seriously. One day I heard a thought that challenged me. A counselor made the statement that many marriages fall apart because of constant scolding and nagging. I understood that statement. I find myself resisting those who are always fussing at me and responding more positively to those who treat me with respect and courtesy. Maybe it *is* true that one attracts more flies with honey than vinegar.

I feel we need to be positive in preaching the resurrection message. If people don't take the faith seriously, they need to hear about the heart of our faith. The gospel needs to be presented in a winsome and attractive way. The truth must be spoken in love. If we are positive in our approach to the story, if we radiate our confidence in it, then we might be able to prepare people to respond to the Holy Spirit. After all, the gospel is *good* news!

Strive for Simplicity

One of the dangers in preaching about the resurrection is that it is such a complex event with such complex meanings that we will preach it in vague and mysterious ways. We do not understand all there is to know about the resurrection. The depths of its meanings we have not begun to fathom. In trying to explain it, we may clothe it in words and ideas that may conceal and confuse it's meaning.

What is amazing about the Bible is that, for the most part, it deals with the resurrection in simple terms. "He was killed, but He rose again." "He is alive." "Christ is risen." Simple words were used to describe that tremendous event. We should strive for that kind of simplicity. If there is one truth we want to make clear to everyone, it is that Christ is alive now and always will be. Since He is, nothing in this world can defeat Him, no suffering or sin or death. For those who trust Him, nothing in this world can ultimately defeat them. As we trust in Christ, He holds on to us for all eternity. In simple words and illustrations, we need to tell that story.

Conclusion

This book shows how I have preached the Easter story. I make no claim to have done it well. Others do it better all the time. I offer these sermons with the hope that they may inspire better sermons and encourage the preaching of the resurrection story. My hope is that what you read will deepen your commitment to the resurrected Christ and keep alive the deep joy and hope of our faith. Together, may we continue to celebrate the presence of Christ here and forevermore and start ringing the rusty bells of hope in the lives of those for whom the music of joy has died.

Series I

A Pilgrimage to Easter

Sermon series are always good ways to preach the truths of Scripture. They usually heighten the interest level of the congregation. Series also help people see that the gospel is a story, each part connected to the other, not just unrelated events.

This series seeks to get the Easter story in the correct chronological sequence. Hopefully, it will make it easier to follow the progression of events that led to the resurrection.

Sermons

Toward Jerusalem: The Ultimate Commitment
Gethsemane: A Struggle of Wills
The Last Supper: The First Celebration
The Cross: The Challenge to Change
The Empty Tomb: Seeing Beyond

1

Toward Jerusalem:
The Ultimate Commitment

Luke 9:51-53

We were taking a hike in the woods and had gotten lost and were trying to find our way back to the main road through all of that brush. We were following a trail that seemed to lead to the way we wanted to go. Then all of a sudden, the trail forked. This way . . . that way—we had to decide. Which road should we take? Which one would get us where we wanted to go? I remember that as we stood there trying to make that decision, how agonizing it was because no matter which one we chose, we didn't know if it would get us to where we wanted to go. But we had to make a choice. As hard as it was, we had to choose.

As we look back on our lives, we can see that most of what we are is the result of decisions we made at the forks of the roads of our lives. There have been many of them. A career is a fork in the road. What will we do with our lives? To choose this career means we can't choose that one. We have to take a risk. Which one will bring us the deepest joy? Marriage is a fork in the road. To be married or not to be married—each has its advantages, each has it disadvantages. Which one will bring us the most fulfillment? We have to choose. To believe or not to believe! That's a fork in the road. Will we live as a Christian or not? We can't have it both ways. We have to choose which one will be best for us. How many times have we wished that we could go back to one of those forks and change our decision? We can't do it. It's too late. We chose, and we walk down that road. We have to live with the consequences of our decision. What we are today is due to the decisions we made yesterday.

The same was true with Christ. Before Easter could happen, He had to choose to let it happen. Those people who lived through the cross-resurrection experiences were not actors who performed roles in robot-like fashion. They were real live human beings who had to choose the way to walk. So did Christ. Would He go to Jerusalem? He knew what going to Jerusalem meant. He knew that if He went He would get into trouble. He knew that if He went to Jerusalem He would die. But He had to choose: toward Jerusalem or away from it, toward His death or toward His own life. Luke 9:51 says, "He set his face to go to Jerusalem." Other translations add the word *steadfast.* In other words, He made a major life decision. He would go to Jerusalem to die; and once He had made that commitment, He would not turn back. Jesus chose to die.

We say, "So what? Why should I be interested in that?" Here's the reason: Christ made the commitment to go to Jerusalem to die for you and me. He did it to help us, to give every one of us a chance to become the kind of person we ought to be. We are the ones who have benefitted from His choice to die. As we begin our pilgrimmage to Easter, let us look at some of the reasons Christ went to Jerusalem and what it means to us.

I. To Bring Us Healing for Sin

When Jesus went to Jerusalem, He went to deal with the poison of sin that was loose in the world. Human beings brought in the power of sin, that destructive evil force, when they decided that they knew better than God how to live their own lives. So they rebelled against God. They did what God did not want them to do. When they did so, sin came into the world. It was a deadly happening, for sin is a fatal disease. The Bible says, "The wages of sin is death" (Rom. 6:23). Inward death, spiritual death, is certainly the result of sin. For once sin comes into our lives, it destroys us inside; it destroys our best qualities. It keeps us from loving as we should. It keeps us from being as good as we should. It keeps us from knowing right from wrong as we should. Sin eats away at our spirits. It eventually keeps us from being what we need to be.

We can't seem to do anything about sin. It is as if the doctor had turned to us and said, "I'm sorry. I've done all I can. There is no more." We try to deal with our sin and the consequences of it. We try to deal with our guilt. I read in the paper that a new idea had been found. It was a guilt bag. People get a bag and blow into it to get rid of all their guilt. Then they throw the bag away. They've gotten rid of their guilt. People were buying the bags. How ridiculous! Guilt doesn't go away that easily. Once sin gets hold of us and we've gone against God, it has a death grip on us; there is nothing in the world that we can do to break it.

Christ chose to go to Jerusalem to take the death that sin ought to be giving us. When He climbed on that cross, He died for you. He died for me. He died the death that sin should give us. But He took it. He wrestled with it. He overcame it. And He said, "Look! Sin did it's worst to me. But I defeated it."

Jesus Christ brings us the cure for our fatal disease; Jesus Christ offers forgiveness. Now the medicine He offers does not remove all the scars and pain of that sickness. We have to wrestle with sin every day of our lives. We have to do all we can to defeat it ourselves. But it will not claim us as its victim if we put our trust in Christ. He died for our sins. The death we deserve, He took.

Paul Mims, who pastors Druid Hills Baptist Church in Atlanta, Georgia, told this story. Jerome was a Roman Catholic scholar who translated the Bible from Greek to Latin, and Jerome's translation served as the official Bible of the Roman Catholic Church for about a thousand years. Near the end of his life, Jerome was living near Bethlehem translating some of the Bible when he had a dream. In the dream, the Christ child appeared to him. He was so overwhelmed by the appearance of the Christ child that he felt he just had to give Him something. So he got some money and offered it, saying "Here! This is yours." The Christ child said, "I don't want it." Jerome brought some more possessions. The Christ child said, "I don't want them either." And Jerome said, "If there is anything in the world that I can give you, tell me what it is. Tell me! What do you want? What do you want me to give you?" He said he dreamed that the Christ child looked at him and said this. "Give me your sin! That's what I came for."

What sin is it that's keeping us from being what we ought to be? Give it to Him! He died to take our sins away, to bring us healing for that which would keep us from being what we ought to be. The best response we can make to Christ is to trust Him with the worst things that we have done and let Him forgive us for them.

II. To Show Us What God Is Like

When Jesus went to Jerusalem and died, He opened the heart of God for all to see. Jesus showed us what God thinks of us. Think of the suffering, the agony of a cross. Why in the world would God go through all of that? I can imagine only one explanation. He must really care for you and me. He must really love us to allow all of that to happen to His Son. Jesus came to tell us that God loves us that much. That may not seem to be such a radical idea to us, but it was to the Jews. Jesus taught them two basic ideas about God that were new.

A. God Is on Our Side.

Since the beginning of time, people have been suspicious of God. In the garden of Eden, the serpent tempted Adam and Eve at that point. "Look, you know why God doesn't want you to eat that fruit? Because if you do, you'll know exactly what He knows. You'll be exactly as He is. He's holding out on you. Don't trust Him." So they began to be suspicious of God and betrayed Him. Job, in the midst of all of his suffering, demanded—and that's the word—*demanded* of God, "Explain yourself! Why did you cause me all of these sufferings?" Job was suspicious of God, suspicious of God's motives. Job questioned Him. And down through the years, countless people and religious philosophies have emphasized sacrifices and good works to please God, placating Him, getting Him to be on their side.

That's a misunderstanding of God. All we have to do is to remember what Christ did for us. See Christ's scars! The scars of Jesus are reminders of the love of God. How can we mistrust the God who was willing to suffer that much for us? Why do we? God is surely not working for our worst; He is working for our best. We don't have to mistrust God at all.

B. God Understands What We Face.

At the cross, Jesus faced all of our experiences: loneliness, suffering, rejection, inward despair, and death itself. He faced it, and He knows it. He understands it. God loved us enough to come into the midst of our experiences and help us to triumph over them. He knows how to do it because He's been there. He's felt our pain.

A man got word that his son was killed in the war, and in anger and grief, he ran out of his house, over to his pastor's house, into the study, grabbed the pastor by the shoulders and cried, "Where was God when my son was killed?" The pastor said to him, "The same place He was when His own Son was killed."[1]

God understands and cares. A little boy sitting at the table didn't want to eat his carrots, which is not surprising. His mother said, "Eat those carrots or go to your room." He didn't want those carrots, so he went to his room. A few moments later, his mother went by the room and peeked in. The little boy was looking in the mirror, with tears coming down his cheeks, singing at the top of his lungs, "*Jesus* loves me, this I know." The little boy may have thought that his mother didn't care but that at least Jesus does.[2]

I know that the God we see in Jesus Christ is the God who loves me. It's a shame it took a death for Him to show me that. But a death was given, and no longer do I have to walk in fear and mistrust of God. I walk in adoration and love of Him.

III. To Show Us that Sacrificial Service Is the Key to Life

Jesus Christ came to teach us how to live; when He climbed that cross, He gave us the key to life. The key is not in getting, but in giving. It is not in being served, it is in serving. It is not in amassing huge fortunes; it is in sharing. It is not in finding life; it is in losing it. It is not in a crown but in a cross.

Most Jews didn't believe that. They believed that life was found in wealth, power, and in a material kingdom. They thought that the Messiah would be a military one who would come and overthrow the Roman government and establish an earthly kingdom. Then the Jewish folk would have the money. They would have the power. They would have happiness. But Jesus said, "No. No, you won't. Material things cannot buy you life. You've got to find something more. You've got to find something worth giving your life for, something that will last, and that is service to the kingdom." Christ came not to be a conquering king, but He came as a Suffering Servant. In giving Himself away, He brought us life.

The same is true for you and me. In giving ourselves away for His sake, we find life. I'm not sure we believe that. On what are we banking for life? The things we can hold in our hands or the love that we can give away to others? The power that we have to control others or the service we can render to meet the needs of others? The positions we have that we can brag about or the witness that we might give for the love of Christ? Which is it? Life is found in service.

Stonewall Jackson was a tremendous general in the Civil War, known to be courageous and brilliant. He was also a dedicated Christian gentleman, a man ahead of his time. He freed his slaves before the Civil War. Before he gave them their freedom, he organized them into a Bible class. He not only taught them the Bible because he was concerned about them as persons but also taught them how to read the Bible so that they would be better able to deal with life as they found it. During the Civil War, Jackson sent many letters home to the pastor of his church. In those letters, Jackson never mentioned a word about how the war was going, never a word of his victories or of his defeats. He only asked about that Bible class of former slaves. How were they doing? What were they learning? He always sent money to help support it. This was what Stonewall Jackson was interested in most. Them! How could he help them?[3]

For whom or what have we given ourselves away? To feed the hungry? To clothe the naked and visit the sick, take the stranger in? To befriend those who don't have friends? To help share the burden of the oppressed and the needy? To stand up to try to right what is wrong? I guess it's an important question for us to answer, and the way we answer it may determine whether we will ever really experience life as we want it. Are we more interested in what Christ can do for us than we are in what Christ can do *through* us for others? Which is it? Christ came to show us that when we give ourselves away we will live.

Christ set His face to go to Jerusalem, and He went. He died . . . for us—to bring *us* healing for our sins, to show *us* that He loves *us,* and to give *us* the key to life and to happiness.

What does it matter that Jesus did all of that for you and me? What difference does it make? Do we care? When Abraham Lincoln's body was being borne through the streets of Springfield, one Negro lady put her son on her shoulders so he could see over the crowd, and she said to him, "Take a good look. He died for you."[4]

What we ought to do as we make our pilgrimage to Easter is to take a closer look at what it cost to bring us Easter. We ought to take a look at this Christ who did it for us. We need to ask ourselves, "So what?" Jesus set His face to go to Jerusalem, to the cross at Calvary. Then came the joy of Easter! May you and I set our faces toward Christ, toward discipleship, so that one day we will all be able to share in the eternal joy of His kingdom.

Notes

1. John Claypool, *Tracks of a Fellow Struggler* (Waco: Word, 1974), p. 35.

2. Herschel Hobbs, "Touching the Untouchable," *Baptist Hour Sermons,* 22 Sept. 1974, p. 23.

3. Theodore Speers, "The Book on the Shelf," *Pulpit Digest,* Nov. 1961, p. 33.

4. Harry Emerson Fosdick, *The Hope of The World* (New York: Harper & Brothers, 1935), p. 230.

2

Gethsemane: A Struggle of Wills

Matthew 26:36-46

Once a year Southwestern Baptist Theological Seminary holds a missions weekend, and college students from all over the Southwest come to it. On one such weekend, we were playing host to two girls from an Arkansas college. In a conversation with one, she asked me, "Tell me. Do you think Jesus ever knew doubt and uncertainty? The reason I asked that question was this: My college professor says no. He says that Jesus could never feel doubt, and He could never feel uncertainty."

That's an interesting opinion. But there's one question I would like to have asked: What does the professor do with Gethsemane? For if I understand it correctly, Jesus wrestled with the will of God at Gethsemane. He knew what that will was. It was a cross and all the suffering and death that went with it. And He didn't want to do it. "If it be possible, let this cup pass" (v. 39). For a moment, at least, Jesus doubted that the cross was the way for Him. For a moment, at least, He was uncertain about the road that He should travel. He wrestled with it. He did not want to do what God wanted Him to do. He struggled with it. His will . . . God's will. But in the end, "Nevertheless not my will, but thine" (Luke 22:42, KJV).

I am glad that verse is in the Bible because Gethsemane is a place where you and I will go more often than we want. For Gethsemane occurs anytime we struggle with the will of God, whenever we have to decide: Will I do what God wants, or will I do what I want?

Gethsemane is a struggle of wills. Who will be first in our lives? It's a struggle of will power. Often we know in our minds what we ought to do, but we don't do it. Often we feel in our hearts what we ought to do, but we don't do it. We have to bring it down to the level of will and *do* what we say we feel and *do* what we think. We have to will it. That's where the struggle comes in. Day by day, the constant fight that we have is with God, whether to do what He wants and be what He wants or not.

As we make our way toward Easter, we're going to have to face up to God and to what He wants from us.

I want us to visit Gethsemane to see what it can teach us about the will of God and about our relationship to Him.

I. The Will of God Is Not Easy

One point that comes out of Jesus' Gethsemane experience is that doing God's will is not easy. What God asks us to do is often hard. What He wanted Jesus to do was terrifying! Jesus recoiled from the suffering and death and loneliness and rejection! He didn't want it. He wanted to run away from it! He fought against it because it was hard and difficult and tough. So intense was the struggle that the Scripture says He sweated as "as it were great drops of blood" (Luke 22:44, KJV). Following God's will was not easy for Jesus. At the end of Jesus' struggle was a commitment to what God wanted. We have benefited from that.

We must understand that when God confronts us with His will, it is not always easy. He makes demands upon us that we don't want to do. He asks changes of us that we don't want to make. As we struggle with what God wants us to do and be, we will have moments when, like Jesus, we will want to run away. Take, for instance, loving our neighbor and loving our enemy. We know He wants us to do that, but it is hard to do. We are not too sure we want to do it. So often we don't.

God calls us to be peacemakers. We know He has called for us to wage war on war. All of us are against war. All of us are for peace. We don't like violence and cruelty. It's not the best way of life. But when we are asked to try to bring peace, to pay the price for it, to work for it, that's a little bit harder. We're not too sure we want to follow God's will.

We know that God wants us to be part of the brotherhood of all humanity. To have that, we have to root out all of our prejudices. We've got to look at them, understand them, and try to get rid of them. That's a painful experience. We have to change our attitudes, and we're not sure we want to do that.

We know that God wants us to change as persons. We need to discipline ourselves to worship, pray, study the Bible, and serve. But those disciplines are time-consuming, and there is so much else to do. So while we know what we ought to do, often we just don't.

What is it that you are struggling with now? You know what God wants you to do, but you don't want to do it because it's too hard. What Gethsemane are you facing today? It will not be easy for you. You will have to struggle. I hope you never get the impression that discipleship is an easy road to walk. It is not. There will be tough decisions, tough experiences, and you will have to wrestle with them.

When I grew up, I got the idea that doing the will of God was easy. When I made my commitment to the ministry, everyone reinforced that idea. They said, "It's wonderful to be a minister. You're going into the best work there is. God will really bless you!" He has blessed me. To share in God's work, to serve as His minister, is a sacred privilege. But along with the blessing go some difficulties. Ministers struggle with wanting to please everyone and knowing that they will never be able to do that. It is difficult to go to bed at night, always knowing that something else needs to be done. It is agonizing to stand in the midst of those suffering with pain and tragedy and have little to say. It is hard to want to help and try to help and see so many go away not wanting to be helped. It is hard, at times, to deal with the thoughtless criticisms of those who are your brothers and sisters in Christ. At times, I wonder, does God really want me to do this? It's a real question. It is not only my struggle.

Here is Tom. Tom feels that God wanted him to be a missionary. But his girl friend says, "No. I'll leave you if you go." His parents say, "No . . . don't go." But he feels God has said yes. What will Tom do? Which price will he pay?

Here is Mary who wants be be popular. To be that, she's being asked to compromise her sexual integrity, and she believes it's not what God wants. What will Mary do?

Here is Mr. Davis who works for a company that wants him to tell half-truths about their product, and he doesn't believe it's honest to do so. But it's the only way he can get promoted and get anywhere. What will Mr. Davis do?

Here is a friend of mine who is told by his church to preach on anything he wants except on race relations. He believes the Word of God has something to say about it and feels convicted to preach on it. But he has a wife and two children, and he needs to eat. What will my friend do?

The will of God does not come to us easily wrapped. It comes with struggle attached to it. To do the will of God is often hard. We have to choose. Which will it be? God's will or ours?

II. The Freedom to Say Yes or No to God's Will

"If it be possible, let this cup pass," Jesus prayed. He wouldn't have prayed it if it weren't possible. Jesus could have said no to the cross. He could have walked out of that garden and away from the cross. He wasn't forced to take it. It wasn't compulsory. He finally chose the cross freely. The cross was willingly taken. It was voluntarily taken. God would not force even His own Son to do what He did not want to do. Jesus had to wrestle with that choice. To say yes and to walk with God or say no and walk away from Him.

You and I have that same freedom. God will never make us do what we do not want to do. You and I have the freedom to say no to God's will. God could have made us like robots who would automatically do what He said and automatically love Him. We would have been like machines, and God did not want that. He wanted love that was freely given. He wanted commitment that was willing. So He made us with free choice. God limited Himself by having to honor the choice that humans made. If we say no to God, He will honor that no all the way through eternity. It will break His heart that we say no, but He will give us the freedom to live in the light of it. If we say no, He will not come down, grab us by the napes of our necks, and shake us until we do His will. However, there is one caution I must add here. Whatever we choose, we have to live with the consequences of our choices. If we choose God's will, we live the consequences of that. If we choose our wills, then we live with the consequences of that. To walk away from what God wants us to do means that eventually we will end up walking away from God and we will lose Him. Whenever we do that, we will be destroying ourselves. When we say no to the will of God, we do not do well.

For instance, we can say no to loving our neighbors and loving our enemies, but when we do, hatred and bitterness will become part of our lives, and it will eat away at our spirits, and it will keep us from ever knowing joy and happiness as we should. We can choose that, but it will hurt us.

We can choose not to be peacemakers. We can give in to force and violence. But we will be living then with fear—fear of another or the fear of a nation. We will live with destruction always around the corner. We will never know inner peace. We can choose that, but we will not do well.

We can choose not to be brothers to one another. We can nurture our prejudices and our bigotry, then we will live in fear of one another. We will live in suspicion of one another. We will never know the fellowship of one another. We can choose that. But we will not do well.

We can choose not to do the disciplines of the spirit. We can ignore prayer. We can ignore worship. We can ignore studying God's Word. We can ignore service. We do that at our peril. It will take away any chance we have to become more than we are.

We can choose no. But to choose no means to live with the consequences of living on the other side of God.

Gethsemane is a very lonely place. No one can choose for you. I can't. Your friends can't. Your loved ones can't. You alone must choose. Which will it be? God or not? An old man lived like a hermit in the mountains of Virginia. He was known for his wisdom, and some of the young folks were always trying to trap him and make him look foolish. One fellow finally got an idea. "I'm going to catch a bird, and I'm going to hold it in my hand. I'm going to say to the wise man, "Is this bird alive, or is it dead?' If he says it's dead, I'm going to open my hand and let it fly away. If he says it's alive, I'm going to crush it, and it will be dead. I've got him now!" So they went to the wise old man, and the boy held the bird in his hand and said, "What have I got?" The wise old man said, "It seems like a bird that you have caught." The boy said, "Tell me . . . is he alive, or is he dead?" The old man looked straight in the eyes of the young boy and said, "It is as *you* will, my son. It is as *you* will."[1]

So it is. God gives us the opportunity to choose life or death, and it is as *we* will. Which choice will we make?

III. God Will Help Us Follow His Will

Jesus left Gethsemane to climb that cross, but He was able to do it because He believed that His Father would be with Him. That was the faith He lived by. God would be there when He needed Him. When He left Gethsemane, it was tough to face pain and suffering and death. But in the end, these last words came from the cross, "Father, into thy hands I commit my Spirit!" (Luke 23:46). He trusted God even with the cross. With God, anything is possible, even that cross.

When you and I are confronted with the will of God, it seems like a mission impossible. Too hard to do! We don't want to do it! We can't do it! It is true! When we see what God asks us to do, it is an impossible task on our own. But we must not forget one thing. God will never ask us to do what He will not help us do. What God says can be done with

His help. All things are possible through Him who strengthens us (Phil. 4:13). Loving a neighbor or loving an enemy . . . impossible? So it seems. Have we ever let Him help us do it? Have we trusted Him to help us to love one another? He is able to. Be a peacemaker? It's hard. Nobody will say otherwise. At times it seems impossible, but have we ever really let Him do it through us? He is able to. Be brothers to one another? Have we given our prejudices over to Him honestly? Have we honestly let Him deal with them? Have we honestly let Him help us become a better person?

The problem is that, most of the time, we haven't let Him help us do His will. We haven't even tried His will. God says, "If you trust me, we'll be able to do what I ask." Now it won't be easy. You'll have to do your part. Christ had to get up and go through all that He had to face; but in the midst of it, God was still with Him. That's the truth He promises to you and me. When we say yes to the will of God, we don't leave Gethsemane by ourselves. We leave Gethsemane with God as our partner.

It's foolish to think we can do the will of God by ourselves, and it is not required. What is required is that we do the will of God with His help. Norman Vincent Peale told the story of a friend, Glen Henderson, who was with a group of mountain climbers climbing the White Eagle Mountain in Canada. The mountain is 9,000 feet high, and they had made it up to 5,000 feet. It was a dangerous mountain. The week before, a ski master had been killed in an avalanche. When they got up to 5,000 feet, the guide said, "Now, we've got to cross this little place right here." It was a very thin place to cross. There were valleys on every side, and it was very steep. One false step, and down they would go. He said, "We've got to be very careful in this particular place. One false step is dangerous. But also noise, a whisper even, could cause an avalanche to come." He took out a big ball of red yarn and cut out lengths of fifty feet and gave them to each one to tie around their waists. He said, "If we happen to be crossing over and an avalanche starts, here's what you do. You throw away your skis and your ski poles and you start swimming, just like you would do in water, trying to get to the top of it. But if you don't make it to the top, this yarn that you will have tied around your waist will. We will be able to find you much quicker when we see the red yarn." Those are not very encouraging words, are they? They're sort of frightening words, scary words. The words were frightening to one twenty-year-old girl. She began to panic. She began to cry. She said, "I can't do it! It's too dangerous! I just can't do it!" Glen Henderson turned to her and said, "Let me ask you this. Has God taken care of you and your life so far? Has He done a pretty good job of it?" The girl said, "Yes, He's done a good job of it." "Well, don't you suppose that you might be able to trust Him for twenty minutes more?" She began to think of all that she had come through and all that she had experienced and how God had, indeed, been of help to her. She said, "You know, I think I can." So in faith, and not in fear, she walked over that dangerous part, no longer frightened, living in confidence of God's help.[2]

I don't know how many times you will stand looking toward some difficult step you have to take. You're frightened. It seems impossible. But hasn't God helped you already? How many nights have you made it through that which you never thought you would? How many steps have you taken you never thought you could take? How many times has God been there? He will not leave us now. If we will trust ourselves to His will, He will help us do it and we just might be surprised what we are able to do.

Gethsemane is a hard place. It's a place where all of us will have to struggle with what God wants. Will we do it? Or will we do what we want? I like the comment of the fellow who got home from boot camp in the navy. He was telling his parents how at the beginning it was quite tough on him, but he made this comment. "Once I made up my mind to let the Navy have it's way in everything, I got along fine."[3]

This is the truth in religion. Once we make up our minds to let Christ have His way in everything, we will be able to get along better than we ever thought. But it's a choice we have to make. Will we do what God wants? We know what it is. Will we do it?

An old monk was asked by a young monk one day, "Are you still wrestling with the devil?" The old monk said, "No, I no longer wrestle with the devil. Now I wrestle with God." "And do you hope to win?" And the old monk said, "No. I hope to lose."[4]

As you and I struggle with God and with what He wants for us, I pray to God that every one of us will lose. When we lose to Him, what we gain is love and joy and life and His kingdom. The only way we will ever gain it is to lose to Him and to come to the place where all of us say, "Not my will, but thine."

Notes

1. J. Wallace Hamilton, *Ride the Wild Horse* (Westwood, N.J.: Fleming H. Revell, 1952), p. 76.

2. Norman Vincent Peale, *Favorite Stories of Positive Faith* (Pawling, N.Y.: Formulation for Christian Living, 1974), pp. 41-42.

3. John Redhead, *Sermons on Bible Characters* (Nashville: Abingdon Press, 1963), p. 44.

4. John Claypool, *Glad Reunion* (Waco, Tex.: Word, 1985), p. 150.

The Last Supper: The First Celebration

1 Corinthians 11:23-25

There was no way in the world for the disciples to know that, when they gathered around the table in that upper room, it would be the last time they would be with Christ before His death. They didn't know it, but Christ did! He wanted to make that supper something special. He wanted to make sure that they would remember. What He did was to give them the gospel for the eye so that, when they saw those symbols, they would remember what He had done for them.

The second time the disciples celebrated the supper was after the resurrection. And it *was* a celebration. Then they knew exactly what Christ had done for them. Whenever they gathered to worship, they gathered around the table to remember what Christ had given them. They celebrated with joy.

On Maundy Thursday evening when we come together around the table, we need to remember that this is a celebration. It is a celebration of God's redeeming us from our sins. It reminds us that we have a lot to celebrate.

I. Celebrate Love

Sacrificial love is certainly symbolized in the Lord's Supper. A body broken and blood shed—for us! Christ died for our sins. He didn't have to. We certainly didn't deserve it. Our rebellion against God was vicious and hard, and it still is. What we do to Him is not good, but still He comes in love to give us another chance at God's love. His love gives us redemption. His love brings us a second chance. His love is willing to climb a cross and die for our sakes. Apart from love, we cannot understand it.

Every now and then, someone cries, "Nobody cares for me." Maybe you and I feel that way. But God cares for us. We can be rejected by every person on the face of this earth and God will still love us. Think of that!

38

The God who created the heavens and the earth, who holds the universe in the palm of His hands, that God thought we were lovable enough to send His only Son to die for our sakes. That's how much God loves us. We can know because of this supper that whatever we've been, whatever we've done, we still have not outrun the love of God. It is available for us if we want it.

Every so often I like to call to mind the life of the Japanese Christian, Toyohiko Kagawa, who spent years of his life in the slums of Kobe. He was a little man without much of a body; one lung was gone through tuberculosis. Doctors in America had told him he couldn't live, so he went back to Japan and said, "If my life is short, it will be full." He went into the slums of Kobe and got a little room where the needy people could get to him. There in the stench of the back streets he lived. One day he went out in the streets to preach as usual. With a small group of people around him, he took his favorite text: the love of God. It wasn't an easy place to preach the love of God—a dismal street, dreary day, sleet and rain falling at intervals to disperse his congregation, and rough men laughing at him. "The little man," they said, "and his funny talk about the love of God! What does he know about God, or what does anyone know whether God loves or not?" It seemed they had the right side of the argument, for even as he tried to answer them Kagawa coughed (a hacking cough), spitting up blood. And they laughed again, now partly through pity. "If God loves," said one, "why doesn't He do something for you? A small wind would blow you over." But the persistent little man lifted his arm, wiped blood from his mouth with his sleeve, and went right on with the story about the great love of God. Gradually, in the cold street, their raucous voices got still, for stealing in on even their pagan minds was the realization that right before their eyes was the proof of what he was saying. A little man was standing in the cold spitting blood and yet loving them enough to be standing there doing it.[1]

Christ hung from a cross for us. We can celebrate His love.

II. Celebrate Hope

Whenever we celebrate the supper, as Paul wrote, we "proclaim the Lord's death until he comes" (1 Cor. 11:26). The disciples had no doubt of the eternal reign of Christ because they had seen what He had done. He had overcome the cross! He had overcome death, sin, and suffering! He was alive, and they knew He was alive! They lived with hope.

We know they lived with hope because no longer did they fear earthly rulers. No longer did they run away from trouble and difficulty. No longer did they fear death. Instead, they believed that there was nothing in this world or beyond that could ever "separate [them] from the love of God in Christ Jesus our Lord" (Rom. 8:38). They faced life with hope, and they lived in some of the most hopeless of times, in some of the most hopeless of situations. But they never gave up hope because they believed Christ had conquered and would always conquer.

We can know that this world is in the hands of God, that our lives are in the hands of God. He knows what's going on in the world. He knows what's going on in our lives. He will not let us be torn from His hands. At times, some of the situations which we are in seem hopeless and difficult. The future looked mighty hopeless on that dark Friday when Jesus was nailed to the cross. It was the end of the world for the disciples. However, on Sunday, they discovered that God was not through, that He was beginning to fashion a world that would be forever. With that hope, the disciples changed the world. With that hope, we can change a little bit of our world. We need to remember that we're in His hands and that nothing in this world can stop us from doing what He wants.

Louis Evans told of a soldier who was wounded on a battlefield. It was night. He could not speak. He could not move. He watched the lanterns of the surgeons who went out to check the soldiers on the battlefield. Finally, a lantern came to where he was and shined down on him. The man said to the others, "I believe that if he makes it to sunrise, he will live." That phrase ran through the life of this man. "If I make it to sunrise, I will live." He looked up at the stars twinkling, hoping to see a glimpse of their fading into sunrise. "If I make it to sunrise, I will live." He began to think of everything he could think of: his wife back home and how when they first dated she had shyly put her hand in his as they walked down the street. He thought of the time when he would be back home again, holding her hand. He thought of his children: what they did and what they looked like, how lovely they were, how they played, and he said, "One day, I will play with them again." He hoped. He clung to the hope of that phrase: "If I make it to sunrise, I will live." All through the dark night, he did not give up his hope for the sunrise, and then it came.[2]

Life is hard for us sometimes. Christ says that if we make it to the sunrise, if we hold on, we will discover a resurrection from all that would destroy us. We must never forget the hope He has brought us!

III. Celebrate Life

The disciples discovered something strange. They discovered that they had power for living *then*. They didn't have to wait to discover the joy of living. They knew it then. Their testimony was simply that God's grace was sufficient for every one of their needs. Whatever they needed, He was there. Whenever they needed strength, He gave it to them. They faced some difficult times. It didn't seem like they would have any reason to be joyful as they were persecuted and tortured. But they knew joy, and they went out singing hallelujahs because He was with them.

What the resurrection means is that we can have life now, not only in heaven but also on earth. Christ came to bring us abundant life, and He meant for us to have it today. He meant for us to start living the joy of it now. He gives us abundant life because He is alive. He does it because He comes to be with us. He does it because He has grace that is sufficient for all our needs. We don't have to sit around longing for "heaven." We ought to wake up to what life is available to us now.

Maud Jackson of Dallas, Texas, was declared legally blind at the age of fifty as a result of a disease of the retina and cataracts in both eyes. For twenty years she lived with her handicap, learning braille and other things that blind people develop to help themselves.

One day Maud was washing the linoleum on the kitchen floor and accidently struck her cheekbone by a sharp, glancing blow on the back of the chair. Four days later she saw movement as she passed her hand before her face. Then she saw a lamp on a table and realized it was on. She could see the hands on her braille watch. Immediately, Maud called her daughter, who came quickly. Maud Jackson began looking at pictures and long-treasured possessions that she'd never seen, including pictures of her grandchildren in Colorado.

Maud's sight had come so suddenly that she was afraid it might be gone again by morning. After her daughter had gone, Maud saw what her apartment looked like for the first time, enjoyed the wonderful colors in her clothes, and in the early morning hours went outside just to look at the moon. Then, by moonlight, she examined every shrub, every flower, every tree in the backyard. She watched the sunrise that morning.

The doctor later explained that the blow on Maud's cheekbone while she was cleaning the floor had caused the cataracts to shift so that they no longer covered the retina. The doctor told her: "This may last the rest of your life, or it may not. Enjoy your sight every minute, every hour, every day."

Maud's friends began taking her to visit every place she had wanted to see for so long. Maud Jackson said, "I will never be able to satisfy my eyes' hunger." Many friends, after hearing of her miraculous experience, confessed that they have begun to observe more fully the beauty of God's world and to give thanks every day for the power of sight.[3]

I wonder what would happen in our lives if you and I really lived with that sense of excitement, believing Christ was in everything we did: in our conversations, in our actions, and in our relationships? I wonder if it would change our lives? I have a suspicion that what we would discover is more of life than we've ever known.

The Last Supper was the first celebration of love, of hope, and of life. When we come to the Lord's table, we come to celebrate love.

> What wondrous love is this, O my soul, O my soul!
> What wondrous love is this, O my soul!
> What wondrous love is this That caused the Lord of bliss
> To bear the dreadful curse for my soul, for my soul,
> To bear the dreadful curse for my soul.
>
> When I was sinking down, sinking down, sinking down,
> When I was sinking down, sinking down,
> When I was sinking down Beneath God's righteous frown,
> Christ laid aside his crown for my soul, for my soul,
> Christ laid aside his crown for my soul.
>
> ....
>
> And when from death I'm free, I'll sing on, I'll sing on,
> And when from death I'm free, I'll sing on,
> And when from death I'm free, I'll sing and joyful be,
> And thro' eternity I'll sing on, I'll sing on,
> And thro' eternity I'll sing on.[4]

Notes

1. J. Wallace Hamilton, *Still the Trumpet Sounds* (Old Tappan, N.J.: Fleming H. Revell, 1970), pp. 56-57.

2. Louis H. Evans, *The Kingdom Is Yours* (Westwood, N.J.: Fleming H. Revell, 1952), pp. 135-136.

3. Maud Jackson, "The Glories I've Seen!," *Reader's Digest,* Sept. 1965, pp. 95-98.

4. American Folk Hymn, "What Wondrous Love Is This," *Baptist Hymnal* (Nashville: Convention Press, 1975), p. 106.

4

The Cross: Challenge to Change

Mark 15:16-20

In 1832, the people of Lancaster, Pennsylvania, refused the use of their schoolhouse for the discussion of the desirability of a railroad for that locality because the school board felt railroads were impossible and a great infidelity. "If God had intended that His intelligent creatures should travel at the frightful speed of 70 miles an hour by steam, He would have foretold it in the Holy Prophets. Such things as railroads are devices of Satan to lead immortal souls down to hell."[1]

A woman was shopping and found a plaque that many of us have seen: "Prayer Changes Things." She bought it, took it home, and put it up in the living room. When her husband came home, he looked at it, tore it down, and said, "I don't want things changed. I like them the way they are."[2]

How typical that sounds! How like us it sounds! People are not exactly fond of changes. We know we need to change, but somehow, we never get around to it. We each say things like, I'm going to lose weight; but I can't. I'm going to stop smoking; but I don't. I'm going to stop drinking; but I never do. I'm going to be a tither; but I never start. I'm going to become more involved in service; but that's as far as I get.

How many times have we known we needed to change what we did or were, but we haven't because it was too hard or too painful? How irritated we get when someone comes along to remind us of our need to change. "Don't nag," we each say. "Get off my back. Give me time." Have you ever experienced moments like that? If so, then you can understand better why Christ had to climb a cross. He had to die because He was calling for change, for new persons, and a new world, and there were those who did not want to change. He asked what they did not want to give, and He kept asking; He kept challenging. He was beginning to become a pain, so they put Him on a cross to shut Him up because if

44

they did that they could stay the way they were and have peace. There would be no more challenge to become what they were not.

As we make our way toward Easter, we cannot bypass Calvary. We have to face it and try to understand it. The cross stands as a challenge to us, a challenge to change, to try to become what God wants us to become, to try to do what He asks us to do. Look at what He was calling for then and see how He is challenging us to change today.

I. To Change Our Understanding of God's Kingdom

The people had been waiting a long time for the Messiah to come. They knew what would happen when He did. After a battle, the Romans would be defeated and the Jewish people would be in charge. They would be the conquerors, not the conquered. They would control the wealth; they would have the power; they would be in charge. How they looked forward to that day!

But then Christ came along and changed all of that. He said His kingdom would not be built out of the things of the world but within the hearts of people, not on wealth or power but love and service, not what we get but what we give. That was new talk to them. They couldn't understand it. They thought in terms of dollars and cents and not in terms of love and forgiveness. They wanted a material kingdom, and when Christ wouldn't give it to them, they got rid of Him.

What kind of kingdom do we want? One church had their hymnbooks donated by a drugstore with the stipulation that the drugstore could advertise in the hymnbooks. They didn't put all their advertisements at the back of the book. Instead, they put them among the hymns. So the church members ran across a hymn like this:

> Hark the Herald Angels sing,
> Beecham's pills are just the thing,
> Peace on earth and mercy mild,
> Two for man and one for child.[3]

We're always getting our faith mixed up in that way. We have a tendency to identify the kingdom or our happiness with some "pill" that will cure all our ills. If we just had—a new house, a new car, a new job, a bigger bank account, a bigger position—then the joy will come flowing. We feel that the material is the way to the easy and the good life.

But Christ said, "No. You've got to change that idea. Things will not bring you what you are looking for." It looks as if we should have learned that by now. There's nothing wrong with things, but they were never meant to be at the center of our lives, only on the edges of it. It's the spiritual values that bring life.

A man built a two hundred and fifty thousand dollar house for his wife down at Virginia Beach. Now it's for sale because they got a divorce. A couple has lived for forty-five years in a five-room house near the railroad tracks. Of those two couples, which found life? It wasn't the houses; it was the people in them.

Too many public entertainers—rich, famous, with everything money could buy—could not buy what they thought would bring them joy so they ended their lives. I've seen a sheet metal worker, a struggling farmer, a schoolteacher of forty years bubbling with life and joy. It wasn't the things they had; it was the persons they were.

Why was it that Christ could hang on a cross and become more representative of life than Pilate with all of his legions? The answer was decided by what dwelled inside of them. That made the difference.

Christ calls us to major on the spiritual and minor on the material, but do we do that? Do we have trouble giving ourselves to Christ and letting go of things and giving them to Christ?

Here is a story about a twelve-year-old who had never seen a real live circus. One day a poster went up at the schoolhouse saying that the traveling Ringling Brothers Circus was coming to a nearby town the next Saturday. The boy couldn't wait to tell his family the good news. "Can I go?" The family was relatively poor and didn't have much money for this kind of experience, yet the father sensed how important this was to the lad. So he said, "All right, I'll strike a bargain with you. If you will get your Saturday chores done ahead of time, I will see to it that you have money to go to the circus." Come Saturday morning, all the work was finished, and the boy stood expectantly by the breakfast room table, dressed in his Sunday best. The father reached in his overalls and pulled out a dollar bill, the largest amount of money the lad had ever seen at one time in his life. He was instructed to be careful and sent on his way.

The boy ran at a trot the whole distance from his farmhouse to the town; and as he got to the outskirts of the village, he found crowds lining both sides of the street. He worked his way through to where he could see what was happening. Lo and behold, coming at a distance was an incredible spectacle: the circus parade! It came by where the little boy was standing, and he could hardly believe his eyes! Here were the clowns, the bands, the cages with the various animals, and as each part of the parade passed by, the boy was more and more enthralled. Eventually, the tail end of the parade came in sight. Bringing up the rear was an old clown with floppy pants, droopy eyes, and a rubber nose. As he moved past where the boy was standing, an unusual thing took place. The boy reached in his pocket, got out his precious dollar bill, gave it to the clown, and turned and went home. What had happened? He thought he had seen the circus when he had only seen the parade![4]

That is a parable that happens to many people. They are taking out the precious dollars of their lives and giving them to material objects as if they were the final treasure, when in fact they are only the prelude to the real thing. Don't let that happen to you. Life is found in the spiritual, not the material.

II. To Change the Way We Live

Christ got into trouble because He was always challenging the people to live better. He was always crying out against their sins, telling them that it mattered how they treated people; that He was concerned about the hungry and the naked and the prisoner and the oppressed. He told them that they should strive for righteous living, that honesty mattered, that justice mattered, and that faithfulness in marriage mattered. He said that they needed to love one another, that prejudice and hatred were wrong, and that they needed to learn how to forgive seventy times seventy. It was important that they learn to be peacemakers and quit pushing others around. After a while, they got tired of listening. Deep down inside, they knew that what He said was true, but the people didn't want to change. They were used to their life-style, and it was hard to break it.

I heard a joke from one of my members about a man who wanted to quit smoking and bought a parrot. The parrot said, "Don't smoke, it's bad for you." That's all the parrot said. Later, a friend met him in the street. "How's your parrot?" Puffing on a cigarette, the man responded, "Oh, I sold him. He was beginning to bug me."

Christ bugged the people because He reminded them of what they needed to do and be, so they got rid of Him. Give those religious leaders credit. They knew that if Christ were right they would have to make some radical changes in their thinking and in their actions, and they didn't want to do that. They got rid of the Judge.

Christ comes as a judge to *us,* calling us to be better than we are. Do we want to? Do we want to become better persons, better Christians? How much? What will we change and what do we need to change?

Many things are not right with us. Hate is wrong. Can we justify it before God? He won't let us be satisfied with it; He keeps warning us against it. Insensitivity to the needs of others is wrong. To pass by on the other side of human need is sinful, and He won't let us forget it. Unfaithfulness to our commitments of love is wrong. He challenges us to keep our vows. Gossip is wrong because it destroys the lives of others. Dishonesty is wrong because it destroys our own selves. What is wrong in your life? What do you do that is keeping you from being the kind of person Christ wants you to be, that hurts your witness to Him, and that causes you guilt? Christ won't condone our sins. He will condemn them.

If we don't want to hear Christ's condemnation, we can ignore Him, try to rationalize away our sins, argue them into oblivion. But He still comes to say they are wrong. Once in Japan, the Imperial Orchestra had one member who could not play a note. The man had influence and wealth. He demanded a place be made for him in the group that played before the emperor. The conductor agreed to let him sit in the second row of the orchestra. He was given a flute; and when the music began, he raised his instrument, puckered his lips, moved his fingers, and went through the motions of playing, but he never made a sound. This continued for two years until a new orchestra leader took over. He required a personal audition by each player. One by one, each member played a solo. When time came for the flutist to play, he was frantic with worry and acted sick. However, the doctor declared him to be perfectly well. He was ordered to demonstrate his ability on the flute. Finally, the man had to confess that he was a fake. He was unable to "face the music."[5]

I can understand how the "flutist" must have felt, for I don't want to "face the music" either. But Christ will one day ask me, "Why didn't you try to change? Why didn't you try to do what I said for you to do?" I wonder, *What will I be able to say?*

III. To Change Our Concept of God

Possibly the main reason the people crucified Christ was that He just wasn't the kind of God they wanted. They wanted a military Messiah, riding into town on a white horse, rallying the people to war. They got the Suffering Servant, riding into town on the back of a donkey, rallying the people to peace. They wanted God to would do what they wanted

Him to do. He became a Savior who called for service to whatever His will was. They wanted God to love the Jews and despise the Romans. They got Christ who loved the Jews and died for the Romans too. He just didn't fit their image of what God should be. Crazy! Dangerous! Radical! Crucify Him! He can't be God!

Down through the years, we have turned against God because He didn't turn out to be the kind of God we wanted. Sigmund Freud wrote a book called *The Future of an Illusion.* In that book, Freud said that God was the product of our imagination, that we needed some idea of a father to help us cope with life.[6] But the flaw I see there is that you and I could have made a better god, couldn't we? Here is a man whose daughter died of lukemia. If he had his way, he would have a god who would not allow such suffering and tragedy in the world. Or here is a woman who's facing disappointment and loneliness. If she had her way, her god would take those things out of life and never allow them to happen. Or here is a boy who prayed to God that his team would win the football game. That's what he wanted his god to be—a surefire guarantor of victory. I suppose a boy on the other team might have felt the same way.

We could do better if we were God, couldn't we? The rain would fall on the just, not the unjust. The righteous would prosper, and the evil would suffer. Anytime we needed God, He would be right there to serve us. For we want a god who will do things our way, do what we want when we want it. But we didn't get and we don't get that kind of god. Instead, we live in a world where there is suffering and tragedy, where troubles don't disappear, where we can lose games even though we pray to win, where the evil prosper and the righteous suffer, where God doesn't always jump when we snap our fingers. Instead, God comes to us and tells us to pick up a cross and carry it, struggle with the burdens and needs of others, expect persecution and suffering. He calls us to live by faith, even in the midst of uncertainty and pain. Have we ever been tempted to give up on God because He doesn't do what we wanted?

My little boy sometimes wanders out into the street and when he does, he gets spanked. He's too young to understand why he shouldn't go out into the street. So he doesn't understand why he should be spanked. At those moments, I'm sure he probably wishes he had another father. He doesn't understand that it was for his own good and for his protection.

We don't always understand the way things go ourselves, but we do understand that Christ went to Calvary to die for our sins because He loved us. We must trust that. We must let Him be the God He is and trust Him with our lives, knowing that in the long run, we won't be sorry.

Easter came by the way of the cross, and that was a surprise. Who would have ever thought it could happen that way? It didn't seem so on that Sunday when He entered Jerusalem, crowds cheering, palms waving, people crying out, "Hosanna! Blessed is he who comes in the name of the Lord!" (Mark 11:9). So He did!

But Jesus asked for too much change from the people. He asked them to major on spiritual values, not material. He asked them to change their style of living. He asked them to trust God and not use Him for their own purposes. And so, "Hosannas" were sung on Sunday, "Crucify him" on Friday (15:13).

Do we do differently? He wants us to change, to become better. Do we chant "Hosannas" in the church on Sunday and "Crucify him" on Friday—or is it even Monday? Whenever we refuse to become what He wants us to, we raise that cross on that lonely hill and put Him to death. Have we trusted Him with our lives? Are we really trying to become what He wants? Are we trying to do our best?

Christ came to Jerusalem to die for us. The crowds cheered until they understood what He wanted from them, that He wanted them to love and serve and become like Him. Then they left! As we remember that triumphal entry into Jerusalem, let us also remember the tragic end and ask ourselves, Will we change and become what He wants?

Notes

1. Eugene Laubach, "Honesty and Integrity," *Sermons From Riverside,* 29 Apr. 1973, p. 8.

2. Ernest Campbell, "Together or Not at All," *Sermons From Riverside,* 3 May 1970, pp. 3-4.

3. J. Wallace Hamilton, *Horns and Halos in Human Nature* (Westwood, N.J.: Fleming H. Revell, 1954), p. 110.

4. John Claypool, "You and Your Treasure," sermon: Broadway Baptist Church, Fort Worth, Texas, 18 Feb. 1973, p. 7.

5. "Face the Music," *Proclaim,* July-Aug.-Sept. 1977, p. 35.

6. Sigmund Freud, *The Future of an Illusion* (London: Hogarth Press, 1928).

5

The Empty Tomb: Seeing Beyond

John 20:1-9

There was a beautiful home in my hometown. It had beautiful land-scaped gardens, pretty grass, and a pond in which goldfish swam. People have told me about the house and gardens. I never saw them because all around that house was a very high, gray stone wall, too high for me to see over. To me, that wall was an ugly thing because it kept me from seeing the beauty that people said was truly there.

In a similar sense, in our experiences of life we come up against many ugly walls that seem to hide the beauty and the joy and the love of life. Such experiences as suffering and disappointment and death rob us of life. We seem to be smashing our heads up against the wall as we try to make sense out of them. Easter speaks to these experiences. For Easter is the reminder that when we come up against those walls that seem to rob us of life, they are not all there is to life. We can see beyond them because beyond is the risen Christ!

Two men laid Jesus in a tomb. A tomb is an ugly thing to us, for it symbolizes death. We fight against death, for it seems to destroy all that we have ever done and all that we have ever been. But the Bible goes on to tell us that the tomb in which Christ had been laid was found empty. He was not there. That was a surprise . . . quite a surprise! Not only to the religious leaders but also to the disciples. They did not expect it.

People through the ages have tried to explain the missing body. Some have said that the religious leaders stole the body, but that doesn't make any sense. For when the movement of Christ was spreading like fire across the earth, all the Jewish leaders had to do was to produce the body of Christ to stop it. But they didn't do it. Some have said that the disciples stole the body, but they literally threw their lives away for the sake of Christ. People don't throw their lives away for the sake of that which they know to be a lie, do they? No! The tomb was empty! Christ rose!

We have come here today not to argue the truth of the resurrection, although I think we could do so with some benefit. But people are not really convinced of the Christian faith by argument. We have come together to celebrate the resurrection. What does Christ's resurrection mean to you and me now? What can we cling to because two thousand years ago, He left that tomb? What does Easter help us see beyond?

I. Beyond Suffering

Suffering was, and is, one of the most disturbing facts of life. Nobody wants it. Nobody really understands it. Why do people suffer? We wonder. So did the disciples. For awhile, Christ seemed to be doing something about it. He healed the sick. He took blindness away and made the crippled walk. Then all of a sudden, Christ Himself was overwhelmed by suffering, undeserved suffering. He had done nothing to earn the crucifixion. He was a good man, the best who ever lived. He didn't deserve the cross. But He got it, and it was hard suffering: nails through His hands and feet, thirst, hanging from a cross, the emotional suffering inwardly that caused Him to cry out, "My God, my God, why has thou forsaken me?" (Mark 15:34). The disciples did not understand. They turned and ran. There was no understanding of the cross. Why should Christ, of all people, have to suffer? They did not have an answer.

We understand what they went through. We have all walked through the valley of suffering. In the midst of it, we have tried to understand. A mother stands by the grave of her two-year-old boy. Just for a moment she had turned her eyes, and he had wandered away from their summer home and drowned in the lake. Twelve months earlier she had buried her husband, a scientist, who, while working on an experiment in a laboratory, was bitten by a poisonous rat and died. She stands there, benumbed by grief, shocked by it all. Who is there to tell her the sense of it all?[1]

I remember vividly hearing John Claypool talk about the experiences he went through when his little ten-year-old daughter was struggling vainly against leukemia. He told of the two weeks that he spent in the hospital when her sickness was in its terrible stages. Both eyes of the little girl were swollen shut, and he said, "For two weeks, I stayed every night but one, and during those two weeks she never slept more than thirty minutes at a stretch. I stood in that room, listening to the moans and the cries of the little girl who was wondering if she would ever be able to make it through the night. Don't tell me that it's easy to praise God from whom all blessings flow."[2]

Suffering. It's hard to understand, hard to deal with. All we can do is grin and bear it and give in to hopelessness and despair because there's no meaning . . . no purpose! Without Easter, we have nothing to say to suffering. But then the Easter message: The tomb is empty! Christ is alive! He has overcome suffering. He has overcome pain. He knows how to do it. He will help us do it.

We don't always understand why we suffer, although we do have some new insights. Sometimes suffering is *redemptive*. Christ's suffering brought us closer to God, and sometimes ours can bring others closer to Him. Some suffering is *instructive*. Some suffering teaches us about God and how to become more sensitive to one another. Some suffering is *disciplinary*. It's a result and the consequences of our sins. If we never had to suffer the results of our mistakes, we would never change our mistakes.

But while we never really get a complete answer to the *why* we suffer, Easter gives us a complete answer to *how* we can deal with it. We can deal with our suffering with the help of Christ. Christ overcame His suffering, and He knows how to help us overcome ours. Just as God did not desert Christ on the cross, so Christ will not desert us in the midst of our suffering. Although it is difficult, and the questions come, when we continue to put our trust and faith in Him, we know that one day we will see beyond it . . . and go beyond it.

John Killinger of Lynchburg, Virginia, told a moving story of a couple he knew. They had a son. He was born mentally retarded. They built a bedroom with glass walls in the house so that wherever they were in their house they would be able to keep an eye on their son. They couldn't leave him alone because of his physical condition. For seventeen years, the mother slept next to the boy with her hand next to his heart so that, if he ever started having trouble breathing, she would be able to wake up and give him artificial respiration. For seventeen years, they lived this way. The day the son died, the mother had gone to the hospital with a neighbor's girl who had fallen from a tree and had hurt her arm. As she was standing in the emergency room of the hospital with the little girl, her husband came in carrying the body of their son. He had tried vainly to revive him. There was the boy lying in peace. The parents wept. But then, notice this, they gave thanks to God for the gift of their son. "For," she said, "he taught us how to love."[3]

How, but for the grace of God, could that be? *Only* with the grace of God can we ever deal with our suffering and see beyond it.

II. Beyond Disappointment

The disciples were really heartbroken when Christ was taken, for they had trusted their lives to Him. They thought He would bring in the kingdom. Now their hopes were gone. Their dreams were in vain. The one they had loved was conquered. They ran into the night, heartbroken, tears running down their cheeks. They had not expected it. They did not want it. They didn't know how to handle it.

Disappointment is something we're familiar with, too, is it not? You may be heartbroken because life is not going for you as you wish it would go. There was a job you desperately wanted, but it did not come to you. You had high hopes for your marriage, but it isn't turning out as you expected. A child you know has turned against you and walked a different road than the one you wished. Someone you cared about no longer seems to care about you.

Disappointments come to us. They knock on our doors, and we answer far too frequently. In high school, the Key Club was the elite club. Anybody who was anybody was a member of the Key Club. I wanted to be a member of that club. I had a friend who nominated me for membership, and I remember the night they were to vote on me. How excited I was! How I looked forward with anticipation to become a member of *the* Key Club. But I wasn't elected. I was voted down. I can tell you that there was a sickness inside me that was terrible to have to deal with. I thought that I would never be able to face anyone again at that school . . . didn't even want to. All through that long, dark night, I thought that disappointment would conquer me.

You know what I am talking about, don't you? Because you have been there too. But we need to hear again the Easter message. The tomb is empty! Christ is risen! There is more to life than just the *down* experiences. There are the *up* experiences too. When the disciples discovered that Christ was alive, they changed from cowardly to courageous. No longer were they overcome with despair. They sang, "Hallelujah! He is risen." No longer did they live in disappointment. They could live in the confidence that whatever they faced Christ would be able to bring them through it. They got up and got back in and kept at it.

This is the Easter message for you and me. In spite of all the disappointments that have come down hard on us, they do not have to overwhelm us because Christ knows how to pull us through them. He knows how to get us up again. He knows how to get us going again. We must turn over all of our disappointments to Him and try to trust Him and keep on going.

One of the interesting events of Lawrence Welk's life came when some members of his band came to him early in his career and said, "We're leaving you. We're leaving you because you are going nowhere. Your music is bad. We're leaving before the ship sinks. And besides," they told him, "you can't even speak good English. And when you dance, you bounce around like a ball." So they left. Welk wrote in his autobiography that that was the lowest day of his life. "I thought I would never be able to go at it again. But then I learned to trust God . . . to keep at it."[4] We know what happened. We know who Lawrence Welk is. But who are those who left? Sometimes the disappointments will hurt us and we will have to fall back on the resources that we know. We must cling to God to help us get back in. Easter tells us we can see beyond disappointment because Christ will care for us.

III. Beyond Death

Being able to see beyond death is the center of the resurrection story. The disciples did not believe Christ would rise again. They thought death was the end. The Jewish people did not believe in an eternal life like we do. Though some believed in a final resurrection, many gave in to hopelessness and despair. We can understand that, can't we? I read once in a newspaper a story of an Arkansas preacher whose mother died. He froze her in ice because he thought she would rise again. Her resurrection would be a sign that Christ was coming again. A couple of weeks later, at the time he felt God said for him to pray, he and two other preachers and his whole church in Arkansas prayed that his mother would rise again. What do you think happened? That's right! She did not rise! We would have been overwhelmed if she had. For we just don't expect it in our day.

Easter is a surprise to us just like it was to the disciples. For us, death seems to be the end of it too. We need to hear the Easter message. The tomb is empty! Christ is alive! He lives! Because He lives, so will we! When the disciples heard that, what a difference it made! Before the resurrection, they had trembled in the face of death; after the resurrection, they looked at Christ's death with smiling faces. The world said to them, "Shut up! Or we will kill you!" And they said, "So what?" No longer did they fear death because they knew that death was not the end.

It was just one more experience of living: they would pass through it and beyond it.

For now, though, we still fear death and fight against it. There was a time when we wouldn't even talk about it. But now we do. Almost every day a new book comes off the press trying to help us to understand and analyze death. Books seek to marshall evidence to prove that there is more beyond. We desperately want to believe there is. The Easter message affirms it is! The witness of the disciples, the witness of the Bible, the witness of millions down through the years is that it is true! Christ lives! He rose from the dead! The tomb was—and is—empty! Because He lives, so can we! We cannot prove that beyond a shadow of an intellectual doubt. It is a matter for faith. But when we commit ourselves to the Christ who overcame death, we will discover that the resurrection story is true to life.

We need to hear what Sam and Betty Moffet wrote. When they had been married for twelve years, Betty got cancer. They believed that she would be healed and prayed that she would. She died. After Betty's death, Sam wrote a letter to all of his friends:

> We believed that she would be healed. We prayed the prayer of faith. But the prayer of faith that heals is the gift of God. But it did help us through the long days of suffering. We lived with confidence and expectancy. Even to the end, we knew that the Lord could heal her. But even when the darkness came in close and cold, the trust remained. For now we know that there is a greater miracle than the miracle of healing. There is resurrection.[5]

We will all face death on this earth. But Christ died so we could see beyond death. We can be like the elderly woman who told her minister, "I've got cancer, and I'm dying. I'm scared to death. But I'm trusting in the love of God." Because of what Christ did, we can be like that man who had etched on his tombstone the words, "Gone away with a Friend."[6] This is the way it will be because of Easter. Death is a doorway that opens to life. The tomb is empty.

What does the resurrection tell us? We can see beyond suffering because Christ has conquered it for us and will help us through it. We can see beyond disappointment because He knows how to overcome it. We can see beyond death because He has defeated it. Do we believe it? That's the question. Until we believe this Easter story enough to live it, it means nothing to us.

A little boy, blind since birth, had surgery to bring back sight, and when he saw everything for the first time he cried out, "Everything is so beautiful. Why didn't you tell me everything was so beautiful?" His father simply said, "We tried to."[7] Christ has been trying to tell us life with Him is beautiful. Even in the midst of suffering and disappointment and death, it can still be beautiful because in the midst of them, we will discover that Christ is with us. Wherever He is, there is life, and it is beautiful. The tomb is empty! He is alive! Hallelujah!

Notes

1. Leonard Griffith, *What Is a Christian?* (London: Lutterworth Press, 1962), p. 174.

2. John Claypool, "Strength Not to Faint" Sermon: Crescent Hill Baptist Church, Louisville, Kentucky, 20 Apr. 1969, p. 4.

3. John Killinger, "There Is Still God," *The Twentieth Century Pulpit,* James Cox, ed., (Nashville: Abingdon Press, 1978), pp. 112-113.

4. Bryant Kirkland, "Dare to Fight Without Armor," *Master Sermons,* Apr. 1975, p. 174.

5. Glenn Ogdon, "Surprise!" *Pulpit Digest,* Mar. 1972, p. 40.

6. Wallace Chappell, "You Are of This World," *Survey,* Nov. 1962, p. 20.

7. William Tuck, *Facing Grief and Death* (Nashville: Broadman Press, 1975), p. 99.

Series II

Passion Week Sermons

In the week that preceeded the resurrection, all the competing forces were brought together and the redemption drama reached a fever pitch. The changing moods, the surprising events, and the contrasting ideas produce exciting preaching material. These sermons seek to capture the insight of Palm Sunday and Good Friday.

Sermons

The Sermon that Was Not Seen (Palm Sunday)
Here Comes the King (Palm Sunday)
The Easy Choice of Barabbas (Good Friday)
Simon of Cyrene: Picking Up that Cross (Good Friday)
A Tale of Two Bowls (Good Friday)

6

The Sermon that Was Not Seen

Luke 19:28-38

What will you see as you go through life? The truth is that we will all see different things because we all look at life in different ways. What I notice, you may not. What I think is important, you may think trivial. What moves me may not move you. We all look at life in different ways and from different perspectives.

Two men stand on the edge of the Grand Canyon. One looks over it and is awed by its beauty, its gloriousness. It is a thing of beauty for him. But another looks over it and is judgmental: it is just "a pile of dirty rocks." For him it is no thing of beauty. They saw the same Grand Canyon, but they saw it differently.

We will understand and enjoy life according to what we see or what we don't see. Take, for instance, this Palm Sunday celebration. Jesus rode into Jerusalem on the back of a donkey, people shouted, waved palm branches, and said, "Blessed is the King who comes in the name of the Lord!" (Luke 19:38) It seemed like a great moment, but we must see it all. A few days later, on Friday, some of the same people who were shouting "Blessed is the King" were probably shouting, "Crucify Him!"

Why the change from a celebration to a crucifixion? It had to do with what the people saw of Christ and in Christ. They were always misunderstanding Him, not really grasping what Christ had come to be or what He had come to do. On Palm Sunday Christ was trying to get the message across to them. In a sense, He was trying to preach a visual sermon of the kind of Messiah He had come to be. Our Scripture text recounts in detail the preparation for Jesus' entry into Jerusalem, especially concerning the animal on which He rode. When Jesus entered Jerusalem on the back of a donkey, He was preaching a sermon in symbols. The sermon was meant to help the people understand the kind of Messiah He was. Unfortunately, that sermon was not seen, and, therefore, a few days later they could crucify Him.

In the midst of all our Palm Sunday celebration, will we see Jesus' sermon? Will we understand who this Christ is who rode into Jerusalem on the back of a donkey? What is this sermon He wants us to see?

I. Messiah: Concerned About the Needy

The people were waiting for a messiah who was to be a king, and a king would come riding into town on a fine horse. That was the animal of a king, *not* a donkey. For all through Scripture, the donkey was a symbol of those who were of the lower class. The outcast, the poor, the needy, and the forgotten—were the ones who rode donkeys. That's exactly why Jesus rode into Jerusalem on a donkey! He wanted to let the people know that He was the God who cares for all people and, especially, the poor, the needy, and the forgotten.

Jesus tried to emphasize that all through His ministry. He was known as the friend of sinners. He ate with them and worshiped with them. Nobody else would, but He did. He healed the blind and the sick and the lame, and often He did it on the sabbath to show that the law was not as important to Him as the people were. If their needs were important, He would go against traditional law to help them. He talked about the judgment in terms of how much people cared for the "least of these," whether they gave food to the hungry, clothes to the naked, water to the thirsty, or visited the prisoner and the sick (Matt. 25). Jesus was interested in the underdog, concerned about meeting the needs of the poor and the forgotten.

The other people didn't want to do that. They wanted a religion that was exclusive, only for the good and the righteous. So they got rid of Christ because they didn't want to care for all people.

In our day, we, who on Palm Sunday cry out: "Blessed is the King who comes in the name of the Lord," how much do we follow Him? Are we concerned about those who are the less fortunate in our day? Are we concerned about the poor and the needy and the hungry all around our globe? Will we sacrifice anything to try to feed them? Are we concerned about those who are being oppressed by the mighty and misused by the others? Do we stand up for their rights? Are we concerned about the orphan or the child-abuse victim or the runaway? Are we concerned about the lonely? Are we concerned about those nobody really seems to care about?

If there is one thing church ought to be, it ought to be a place where people care for one another and where people care for the fortunate and the unfortunate and will go outside its walls to minister to them. If we don't care for the people Christ cared about, we have misunderstood Him.

We don't have to care. We can choose to ignore other people. On the eve of the French Revolution, the bishop of Nancy preached a powerful sermon, and Louis XVI was in attendance. It was a sermon on the plight of the people of France, the sufferings they were going through, and the injustices they were facing. If only Louis XVI had heard that sermon and sought to do something about the situation of the people, he might have avoided a revolution. Instead, Louis XVI, who had had a good supper that night, slept and snored all the way through the Bishop's sermon.[1]

We can sometimes be like Louis XVI. We have in our hands the compassion and some of the means to meet the needs of others. But compassion and means have little significance if we do not think using them to meet the needs of others is important. When we wave our palm branches at Christ, are we willing to do what this Christ wants, to minister to the least of these whatever their needs? Leonard Broughton was a preacher at the Tabernacle Church in Atlanta. Some years ago in a poor section of Atlanta, the water became infected, and four people died. A city council meeting was held and members talked about trying to do something to clean up the water in that particular part of town. They tabled the problem for further study. At the same meeting, they approved fifteen thousand dollars for some improvements of a road in front of an influential member's home. That angered Broughton, and he invited the council members to a service the next day, and some attended. For fifty minutes he preached a sermon in which he said that Christ is not only interested in what is inside a person but also what affects a person. Christ is not only interested in saving souls but also in good water for people to drink. They got the message, and at ten o'clock the next morning, money was appropriated so that the water could be cleaned and lives could be saved. Broughton said later, "I baptized seventy-five people in the next few months, and almost everyone said that what got them interested in the church and in God was the fact that they were concerned about giving them water that was good to drink."[2]

We ought to be concerned about all the needs people have; and if anyone should care, it ought to be those who are the children of the Messiah who rode into Jerusalem on a donkey, saying, "I love them. I am one of them." Are we?

II. Messiah: Man of Peace

The Jews had been waiting for a messiah to come, but they had it all figured out what He would be like. He would be a military messiah, riding in on his fine white horse, waging war against the Romans, defeating them, and putting the Jews in power. That's what they were waiting for. Instead, Jesus rode into Jerusalem on the back of a donkey, throughout the Bible a symbol of peace and humility. That was the message that Christ wanted them to see. He had not come to be a captain of war, but the Prince of peace. He had not come to wage war on earth, but He had come to set loose into the world the power of love that could end all wars. He had come not to build an earthly kingdom, but a kingdom where swords would be beaten into plowshares and where the lion and the lamb could lay down together in peace. That is the kind of Messiah He came to be, one not bent on war but one bent on peace.

Jesus has called us to be peacemakers. *Peacemaker* literally means to "wage war against war." Is there any more crucial moral issue of our time than the question of peace and war? We live in an uncertain day, and many of our young people are afraid of the future. They feel there will not be a world for them in the days ahead. Will it be true? I saw what was called a cartoon. A man and a boy were standing in the middle of a bull's eye. The bull's eye had three signs. One sign said, "Ground zero, vaporized." Another sign said, "Two miles away, you're still dead." The third sign said, "You're five miles away, you're cooked to death." The man asked the boy, "What do you want to be when you grow up?" The boy said, "Alive, if it's not too much trouble."[3]

Will it be too much trouble? It will be trouble. It's trouble to try to work for peace, to see the importance of trying to do something about the hatred that lives between nations and peoples. We need to see the seriousness of the world in which we live. No longer are we playing with bows and arrows, but we are playing with power that can destroy us at a moment's notice. On November 25, 1959, in Omaha, Nebraska, at 4:52 AM, a green light went on in one of the computers, and within a matter of twelve minutes, 740 strategic air command bombers were ready to take off loaded with their nuclear payloads. Only in the last couple of minutes did they discover that a malfunction in one of the computers had caused that green light to flash.[4]

This is the frightening thing: so much power under the control of machines, and so many machines under the control of people who are imperfect and sinful. It's a frightening situation, and we, who are God's children, ought to try to do something about the insanity of stockpiling more and more power to kill. We should be trying to do something to end the causes that produce war. Jesus came to be the Prince of peace, to try to bring peace between us. Will we work for that?

Willie came in and said to his mother and father, "I'm doing a paper on what causes war. What caused World War II?" The mother said, "The Germans invaded Belgium." His daddy said, "Well, that's not exactly all there was to it." The mother said, "He didn't ask you, he asked me." "If you're going to tell him, you ought to get all your facts straight and not tell him fairy tales." "Who told you to interrupt anyway? That's always your trouble, interrupting." They got into an argument, tooth and nail. Willie said, "Thank you. I think I know what causes war."[5]

That's the way it usually is. People cannot learn to get along with one another, cannot learn to live with one another; Christ brings the power to help us to do that. He helps us love one another, and we need to be practicing that power and trying to live that way of peace in the places where we are. Maybe it can spread out from us and beyond us. If any ought to be working for the cause of peace, it ought to be those of us who are the disciples of the Prince of peace.

III. Messiah: King of Kings

Naturally, when Jesus entered Jerusalem on the back of a donkey, the people remembered the prophecy of Zechariah: "Your king comes to you;/triumphant and victorious is he,/humble and riding on an ass,/on a colt the foal for ass" (Zech. 9:9). When they worshiped Him they said, "He is the King." Jesus was saying in fact that He was, indeed, the King that He was not the kind of king they were expecting. He was not a king whose kingdom was based on power and wealth, but He was the King of a kingdom that was based on love and joy and brotherhood and peace. He was to be a universal King, and no other kingdoms would last before Him. But Jesus' kingdom would be based on His values and on His terms. The people didn't want that. They wanted their kingdoms right then. They did not want to wait. They did not want to put their trust in peace or love or hope or faith. They wanted it in what they could hold in their hands. They had no patience, so they did away with Him.

How much patience do we have? Are we willing to work with patience and to wait with patience for the coming of Christ's kingdom? Will we dedicate ourselves to what it is Christ says matters most? Will we believe Him when He says that love will overcome hate, that good will overcome bad, that life will overcome death, and that the material is not as important as the spiritual? Do we believe that enough to give our lives to it and to be patient to work for it? Will we believe that His kingdom will come and that, when He rode into Jerusalem on the back of a donkey, He was right? He was the King coming into town. Even though the people crucified Him, they could not stop Him from being King. His kingdom is the only one that will last. Do you believe that? Understand that? Trust that?

I enjoyed that story that Perry Biddle, Jr., the Episcopalian priest, told of the time when he spoke in a church in England. The point of Biddle's message was "the Lord God Omnipotent Reigneth." In fact, he used that phrase several times in his sermon. Each time he used it, he spoke a little louder so that the last couple of times, he almost shouted out that phrase, "The Lord God Omnipotent Reigneth." As people were going out after the service, two ladies came to speak to him. The officer of the church said, "Now these two ladies are mostly deaf, they probably didn't hear much of what you said." One lady came and said, "I didn't hear much of what you said today, preacher. The only thing I heard was that 'The Lord God Omnipotent Reigneth.'" As she went out of the door she turned and said, "But I guess that's all that really matters, isn't it?"[6] Do you believe it matters? That in the end Christ is King?

Christ rode into Jerusalem on the back of a donkey saying, "See me, see what I tried to say to you? I am the Messiah who cares for the poor and the needy. Will you? I am the Messiah concerned for peace, will you be, too? I am the Messiah who is King of all kings. My Kingdom will triumph. Will you believe that?" And the crowd said, "Blessed is he that cometh in the name of the Lord" (Matt. 21:9, KJV). But then they turned around and said, "No, we don't want you. We don't see what you see." So they crucified Him.

Sometimes we can hear a lot about Jesus, learn a lot of ideas about what He wants; but as He rode Jerusalem on the back of a donkey, He showed us. The question is, Will we see enough to follow Him?

Paris was surrounded by the Germans. The French general Gallieni had a plan that could have saved Paris from the Germans, but as he tried to go to the chief commander, a man named Foch, he was stopped by a junior officer. For security reasons, Gallieni was not wearing his general's uniform but the uniform of a private. He told the junior officer who he was, but the junior officer would not even listen to him. He had the general thrown out. Later, he told Foch about a man named Gallieni who had tried to come in to see him. When he heard that, Foch went into a rage, "Why did you turn him away?" The junior officer said, "But who would take seriously a man dressed up like that?" Foch said, "That man had a plan that could save the city of Paris and the lives of a million men."[7]

Christ comes to us today not looking like a triumphant king, but there is no other one like Him. He has a plan to save our lives now and forever more. He has a plan to make this world a better place. He has a plan to make your life and mine better. If only we will see Him for who He is. He *is* the One who came in the name of the Lord. Do you believe Him? Trust Him? Will you follow Him?

Notes

1. Harry Peelor, *Angel with a Slingshot* (Nashville: Abingdon Press, 1961), p. 65.

2. Foy Valentine, *Citizenship For Christians* (Nashville: Broadman Press, 1965), pp. 87-89.

3. "Is the World Ready for Christmas," *Dynamic Preaching* (Feb. 1986), p. 1.

4. Gerald Kennedy, comp., *My Third Reader's Notebook* (Nashville: Abingdon Press, 1974), p. 43.

5. Leslie Weatherhead, "Questions They Asked," *Pulpit Digest* (Sept. 1958), p. 88.

6. Perry H. Biddle, "The Important Point," *Christian Ministry* (Sept. 1982), p. 19.

7. Leonard Griffith, *Illusions of Our Culture* (Waco, Tex.: Word Books, 1969), p. 51.

7

Here Comes the King

Zechariah 9:9

In the Book of Zechariah are written these words:

> Rejoice greatly, O daughter of Zion!
>   Shout aloud, O daughter of Jerusalem!
> Lo, your king comes to you;
>   triumphant and victorious is he,
> humble and riding on an ass,
>   on a colt the foal of an ass (9:9).

I've never seen a king in my life. The closest I've gotten is a president. I did see former President Jimmy Carter. I didn't get Carter's autograph. I didn't get that close. Too many people were around him, pushing and shoving, trying to get a view of him, to shake hands with him. Not liking crowds, I stayed out of that, but I was quite excited about the opportunity to see somebody I had seen so often on TV.

I can better imagine now what it might have been like on that Palm Sunday when Jesus came riding into Jerusalem. Crowds were cheering, pushing and shoving to get a glimpse of Him, putting down palm branches, and shouting "Hosanna." The people were welcoming the King. At least, they hoped He would be the king, the one who had come to town to overthrow the Roman government and set up an earthly kingdom. So they were shouting. They were excited.

That brief moment in the life of Christ was very important. Here comes the King! But what kind of king? These people who were crying out "Hosanna" would cry "Crucify Him" a few days later because He did not turn out to be the kind of king they wanted. Zechariah, the prophet, told about this experience years ago. What kind of king did Zechariah have in mind? What kind of king is Christ anyway? We talk about Him being our King, our Lord, but we better be sure we understand what He is like. Here comes the King!

I. The Seeking King

When a man is a king, he has power. He can tell people to come to see him; he doesn't have to go see them. The president can ask individuals to come to see him at the White House, and they come when he calls. Very seldom does he go out of the White House to see individuals. But Jesus is a different kind of king. He is not a king who stays where he is and calls people to come to Him. He is the King who came seeking people who needed Him.

God created Adam and Eve and gave them a paradise to live in, but they didn't want it. They didn't want to live God's way. They wanted their way, so they rebelled against Him and brought upon themselves the consequences of sin. Like Adam and Eve, we have rebelled against God. We have tried to overcome the consequences of sin through rituals and sacrifices and deeds; but like a child lost in the forest, every path taken leads deeper and deeper into the woods. We have been lost beyond recovery, so it seemed.

But God came down in the form of Christ, leaving behind His heavenly home to walk upon this dusty earth to look for us in the midst of our lostness, to go wherever we were, to do whatever He could to let us know that He still cared and wanted us to be His children. I'm not sure we understand that. Many religions of the world do not understand that. We have the idea that we have wronged God and, because we have wronged God, He has turned His back on us and doesn't want to have anything else to do with us. So we want to know what do we have to do to get back to God. What ritual? What prayer? What deed can we do to get God to like us again?

Have you ever felt that God was against you, not on your side? Have you ever felt that you did not have a chance with God? The prophet Zechariah said, "Your king comes to you" (v. 9). On that Palm Sunday, He came into Jerusalem for the purpose of doing what was necessary to come to us, to tell us that He loves us, to tell us that He is willing to forgive our past sins, and to tell us that He is willing to bring us into His kingdom again if we will only want it. God would go anywhere to tell us that; He would do anything, even if it meant a cross on Calvary.

A daughter ran away from home to the city and lived a life of shame. Her brokenhearted mother went after her. She searched through all of the dives and bars in the city looking for her daughter. In every place, the mother left a snap shot of herself, taped to the wall with a simple message. "I love you. Please come home." She could not find her daughter. But one day, her daughter stumbled into one of those dives and happened to catch a glimpse of the photograph on the wall. She went over and read the message. "I love you. Please come home." She remembered that somebody did care for her. Somebody loved her. She got the courage to go back home, into the arms of her mother who was ready to love and forgive and accept her daughter home again.[1]

So God has come to us, ready to love and accept us and forgive us. If we want to go back to where He is, He will meet us on the way. He's looking for us now to tell us He wants us to be His children.

II. The Triumphant King

Zechariah said, "[He] comes to you triumphant and victorious." The people hoped He would be their messiah and establish a physical kingdom. Jesus was the Victor, but not the kind of victor they thought. He came telling them, in effect, "I'm not building a kingdom on material values but spiritual ones. I have not come to rule the territories of men, but the hearts of people. What is most important is what is on the inside of us, not what we hold in our hands on the outside." That's the kingdom that Christ came to conquer. The values of that kingdom are love and brotherhood and peace and forgiveness. He said such values will triumph. He rode into Jerusalem and hung on that cross triumphant, believing that what He did was right and would always be.

We have a hard time believing it. When one talks about the values of Christ in this world, they seem to be a joke. Take *love*. We don't find many caring people today. We look at the fact that fifty percent of American marriages end in divorce. We have not learned to love one another in the most intimate relationships of life. *Love* seems to be disappearing from our experience. What about *brotherhood?* Prejudice, bigotry, and misunderstanding still exist among nations and classes and races. We do not know one another. We do not understand one another. And I'm not too sure we really want to. Do we want *peace?* The Bible says that one day the lion will lay down with the lamb. We think that is a ridiculous idea in our world, a world where wars break out all over the place, a world that has nuclear stockpiles which defy the imagination. Do we practice *forgiveness?* We want to be forgiven, but how hard it is to forgive. Most of us live lives which are torn apart by bitterness and resentment and grudges that we have not learned to let go.

God's kingdom doesn't seem to be winning, but the message of Palm

Sunday and Easter and the gospel is that His kingdom shall win. When all is said and done, all other kingdoms will tetter and fall before Him. The values that will triumph will be the values of the Prince of peace.

Do we believe that? If we do, we will bet our lives on it. If we do, we will go about this world practicing these values, living by them even though everyone else says doing so is ridiculous. We will bet our lives on love and peace and brotherhood and forgiveness. David Read, a Presbyterian minister, was captured at the beginning of World War II. The Germans made fun of him, saying England would fall in fifteen days. One of them said, as he recognized Read's collar of a chaplain, "This is a new day. The day of the Christian faith is dead. The day of the superiority of the Ayrian race has come. Your day is gone."[2] We can look back on that and say he was wrong. The Christian faith has not died, but the idea of the superiority of the Ayrian race has diminished.

Many kingdoms have been built which proclaimed to be the ultimate kingdoms, but history has recorded their demise as they have fallen to pieces. But one kingdom stands. Christ came into Jerusalem, followed not by armies ready to fight but by disciples with a message of love and hope. He and His kingdom shall triumph.

III. The Appealing King

Jesus entered Jerusalem on a donkey, and that surprised the people. Donkeys were not associated with military men, and they thought Christ was to be that, but He was not. Christ rode into the city on a donkey, a lowly animal, a symbol of humility, a symbol of peace. By that, He was saying that the kingdom of God comes not by force but by love. He would never force anyone to follow Him; He would never force anyone to believe in Him. He would invite them, encourage them, and try to persuade them through love.

We need to understand that. We talk about God being all-powerful. He can do anything He wants to do. That power is might. But that's not true. Power is the ability to accomplish one's purposes. One needs raw brute power to drive a nail, but one needs a different kind of power to mold a mind. You need the kind of power that seeks to inspire and teach others. What was the purpose of God? The purpose of God was to bring life that was abundant and forever for us. How could He accomplish that purpose? He had the choices. God could try to force us to take it, bang it into us. He could have tried that, but He didn't. Instead, He tried the way of persuasive love.

Enter the cross! This is the way that Jesus Christ used His power: not to bash our heads in but to try to love us to death, to love us in such a way that we will be moved to follow Him. We talk a lot about motivation. People tell me we need to motivate people. What we have to do is try this program, or this gimmick, to motivate them. I rebel against that because I think there is only one motivation for Christian service. There is only one motivation for being a Christian. There is only one motivation for discipleship.

The one motivation is the cross and the love that Jesus showed there. If that doesn't mean anything to you, if that doesn't speak to you in your innermost depths, then nothing I can say or do will ever get to you. That's the way Christ chose—the Suffering Servant, not the powerful warrior. He still does it that way. I cannot make you Christian. I would not want to *make* you Christian. All I can share with you is the persuasive love of God and hope you will choose Him. No one has loved us like He has.

In Scotland, there is a lighthouse called Old William's Light. The man who kept the light went into town two times a week to get groceries and go to church. One day he didn't show up at his regular time, and some friends were worried. There had been a very bad storm the night before, so they went to the lighthouse and found the man unconscious. He had slipped on the rocks and had broken his leg, but he had known that the light needed to be lit. He had agonizingly crawled up those long winding stairsteps to the top to turn on the light. Because of his weakened condition, he caught pneumonia. His friends took him back to the hospital, but it was too late. He died. After the funeral, a captain came out and said, "I want to erect a monument to this man." "Why is that?" the friends asked. "Because I was a captain of a ship that night and was caught in the storm. I did not know where I was and I was headed for the rocks. Then the light came on and I was able to see where I was." He said, "This is the first time in my life I can truly say somebody died that I might live."[3]

He was wrong. Two thousand years ago on that hill called Calvary, Christ died so that captain could live, so you could live, so I could live. Christ died for us! Do you understand that? Do you know what it means? Christ the King climbed a cross for you and me.

Here comes the King! Many kings come today, kings of wealth and pleasure and power and might. They say, "Follow me, and we will conquer the world." But let me tell you, any earthly king you follow will fail you. Only Jesus Christ will not fail. He is the King of kings and Lord of lords. Only He will be King forever!

Notes

1. John Redhead, *Getting to Know God* (Nashville: Abingdon Press, 1954), p. 59.
2. David H. C. Read, "Supremacy of the Gospel," *The Pulpit,* Mar. 1956, p. 7.
3. Hoover Rupert, "What Can Lighten Your Darkness"? *Pulpit Digest,* July-Aug. 1981, pp. 32-33.

8

The Easy Choice of Barabbas

Mark 15:1-15

She is a woman in her late thirties. When she grew up, she was a very active part of the ministry of her church. She sang in the choir, taught a Sunday School class, attended missionary meetings, tithed, visited, and helped people. She gave a warm and moving testimony. That was the way it *was*. Today, it is different. Very seldom does she go to church. No longer does she sing in the choir or teach or visit or serve. Now she is one of those many people that the church can label "missing in action."

When I hear stories like that, the first thought that comes to my mind is, *How could she?* With all that she had done and had experienced and had known, how could she turn and leave it all behind? What went wrong? Could it ever happen to me? I deal with religious matters, and I do so because I believe in them, but could a day ever come in my life when I could leave it all behind and no longer be concerned about it? I know preachers who have done that. They have left the ministry; it doesn't matter to them anymore. Could it ever happen to you? Some people who were vital and active members of this church no longer serve with us. They don't sit in these pews or in the pews of any church. They are no longer actively involved. For some reason, they have given it up and left it all behind. Years from now, will that be said about you?

The Bible emphasizes that we must continue to be faithful to our faith. We must persevere. We must run the race to the very end. If we're not careful, we can be unfaithful. This is one truth in Luke 15:1-15. It was the last week of Jesus' earthly ministry. On Sunday, He had gone into Jerusalem and was greeted by the praises of the crowds. "Blessed is he that cometh in the name of the Lord" (Matt. 21:9, KJV). That was Sunday. Now it was early Friday morning. Jesus had been arrested. Pilate had Him. As was the custom during Passover, Pilate would release one prisoner. He gave the people a choice. "Here is Jesus, the one you call the 'King of the Jews' and here is Barabbas, a violent man, a murderer. Which one do you want me to release to you?" That's not much of a choice, is it? And the crowd cried out, "Barabbas." How could they? We need to try to understand the people's reasons because maybe they are the same reasons that cause us to leave behind that which we once thought was right.

I. Peer Pressure

The religious leaders were dead set against Jesus. They had planted several of their own men in the crowd that morning to cry out "Barabbas." The Scripture tells us that the chief priests "stirred up the crowd to have him release for them Barabbas instead" (v. 11). That is heavy artillery. The chief priests were the respected leaders of the faith. The people had listened to them and had believed them. They said Jesus was wrong, and all around the people were crying out, "Barabbas." It's not hard to understand why the crowd joined in. Who wanted to go against popular opinion? Who wanted to be different? It seemed right to join the crowd in order to get along with everyone.

I can understand that. I have been in situations where I have felt peer pressure to become what people wanted me to become and do what people told me to do, to let others run my life. I have often wanted to do it in order to win popularity and acceptance. Haven't we all felt that pressure? Three teenagers in the Dallas jail all told the same basic story. At an early age, they began crime. Two were up for attempted murder and investigation of murder, one for a series of crimes. They said the same thing: They entered a life of crime in order to win the approval of their friends.[1]

Have we ever given up something in order to win the approval of friends, to become part of a group? Did you know that most people who become involved in drugs and alcohol do so because of peer pressure? As one young teenager said, "Everyone else was, so why not?" Many alcoholics and drug addicts took their first drink or first fix because of peer pressure. I know of a young girl who was part of a group who wanted to go to the beach on Sunday. She went to church and couldn't go. The others never went to church, so it wasn't a problem with them. They called her a "square," and it hurt her. She begged her parents, "Please let me go this time." Her parents gave in, and away she went to the beach that Sunday, then another Sunday and then another. Soon church was left behind in order to be a part of the group. People in some groups make statements that pressure us: "It's all right to be religious, but don't take it too seriously." "Sunday School is for kids." "Christian morality is old-fashioned."

How many times have we compromised our Christian values and beliefs on the altar of conformity? How many times, in order to please those who really don't care about our faith, have we compromised and given in on our beliefs? How many times have we denied what we stand for to get along?

A study on peer pressure was done at the University of Stanford. Six campus leaders, those most responsible for shaping student opinion, were put in a room with twenty-four others. Three lines were drawn on a board. Beforehand, the researchers had told the six leaders to tell the people that the shortest line was really the longest. The students were asked which was the longest line? The six leaders were first to answer, and all of them said that the short line was the longest. Out of the remaining twenty-four, only one student said, "No, that's not right." The other twenty-three went along.[2]

We need to resist peer pressure that compromises our Christian faith. When others are crying out no, we might need to cry out yes. When others are crying out yes, we might need to cry out no. When others cry out "Barabbas," we need to cry out, "Jesus!" One student in college had gotten into trouble and stood before the dean. He gave an excuse that there were not ten people on the campus who wouldn't have done what he did. The Dean said, "Did you ever consider that you might have been one of those ten?"[3]

II. Unfulfilled Expectations

The Jewish people had been waiting for a Messiah to come and deliver them from their suffering and their oppression. They had high hopes that Jesus was the One. On that Sunday, they could sing those messianic songs, "Hosanna to the Son of David: Blessed is he that cometh in the name of the Lord" (KJV). Maybe Jesus was ready to act, to do what they expected Him to do—to overthrow the Romans and set up a material empire on earth. But He didn't do it. He didn't show any power. He didn't start a war against the Romans. He put no material kingdom at their fingertips. So they got angry. They could cry out, "Crucify Him," on Friday because Jesus didn't do for them what they wanted Him to do. They were very disappointed in Him because He would not be the messiah they wanted.

Has Jesus ever disappointed you? That's a serious question, for I know persons who have given up the faith because they felt Christ disappointed them. I know a family who had a little child who became sick. In spite of all they did, the child died. From that moment, they had nothing more to do with God, for God was not supposed to let such things happen to them! When it did, they left Him behind.

I know a man who became a Christian and expected life to fall into place for him. No struggles, no problems, but it didn't turn out to be that way. He had problems to wrestle with, struggles to deal with. Life was not a bowl of cherries. That wasn't the way he thought it should be, and he turned his back on his faith.

I have known others who have just gotten tired of serving without seeing any results. They talked, but no one seemed to listen. They visited, but no one came. They fought against wrong, but it didn't seem to disappear. They grew weary of well doing and began to feel that it was all a waste of time. Frustrated and tired, they left it behind.

We can easily cry out "Barabbas" instead of "Jesus" if Jesus doesn't live up to the expectations we have of Him, if Jesus doesn't do for us what we want Him to do. But what we miss is the fact that Jesus did not come down to give us what we want but to give us what we *need*. We need love, and He brings that. We need to know that we have worth and value, and Jesus tells us we do because we are created in God's image. We need forgiveness for mistakes we have made, and Christ brings forgiveness. He comes to give us power in the midst of sickness and frustration and even the presence of death. We find that inner strength to go on because He brings us power.

Christ knew that material kingdoms and physical health are only temporary. They are here today but gone tomorrow. What matters is what is eternal and spiritual, and that's what He came to give us. He came to bring us those values that will not decay by time: faith and hope and love. He came to make out of us a new creation. But He came to do it through a cross. Who wants to look at that? A cross of death and suffering and shame: why that doesn't look as exciting as a man like Barabbas, so strong, such a man of action.

A reporter for a great Chicago newspaper had an interview with Gipsy Smith, the famous evangelist. Something in the interview recalled to the evangelist the occasion when two hundred girls from the red-light district had invaded his meeting. As memory cast its spell over the old evangelist, he detailed the appeal he made to those girls that they might forsake their sins and accept the forgiveness of a loving Christ.

It was all so natural, so unplanned, and so simple that the interviewer forgot that he had come for a story. He seemed to feel himself following the sinners down to an altar of repentance. A tightening gathered in his throat, a mistiness suffused in his eyes, and he was almost at the point of crying out with the Philippian jailer: "What must I do to be saved?" when he suddenly remembered. He was a reporter, not a penitent. He must not let this thing get him. He had a deadline to meet.

Thrusting his best self down in the muck and the mire and scribbling hurriedly to compose his mind, the reporter snatched up some of the glowing sentences of the evangelist and hurried back to the office. In the story that appeared was this sentence, "Ten minutes more, and he would have had me." Think of it. He managed to escape a great spiritual experience by ten minutes. He refused to hold his greatest moment in high respect!4

Jesus has come to bring us a way of life, but He won't give us what we want; He'll give us what we need. Will we let Him? Or will we turn away?

III. Too Busy to Care

How many people were gathered outside of Pilate's residence that Friday morning? My guess is that there were not too many. We know that Jesus didn't have many followers there. The disciples had already fled. Where were all those who shouted for Him on Sunday? Where were all those He healed and who cast their lot with Him?

My feeling is that they were elsewhere, busy about other things, maybe important things. It was Passover, and many were probably in the Temple making sacrifices for their sins. Many had to be at work, struggling to survive. Maybe some were spending time with their families. All these are good things. But Jesus ended up being crucified on a cross, and not many noticed or cared to notice. Many were too busy doing other things to really notice what was going on, too busy doing what they thought was most important while Christ was shuffled off to Calvary.

That happens to us. We are busy people, scurrying to and fro, doing so much. Many of us are like the muck raker in Bunyan's *The Pilgrim's Progress*. He was raking up muck and sticks and needles. An angel came with a crown to put on his head, to invite him into the joy of the heavenly kingdom, if he would only look up, but he was too busy raking up his sticks and his muck to even notice.5

Often we are that way, busy doing good and important things but not busy doing the best. We get involved in clubs and groups that have good purposes, and we ought to be involved in them. But often our clubs interfere with the worship of God through the church. We get involved in our families, and well we should. We ought to take care of our families, but if we really care for our families, we will not neglect the worship and ministry of the church that helps families. We get involved in our jobs, and we have to, but why do we work? What is it for? When our work becomes more important than our faith, we are in trouble. School activities are very important too; but while we grow mentally and physically, we must never neglect to grow spiritually.

When the nominating committee asks people to serve in positions in our church, the answer most often given is, "I'm too busy." Busy doing what? That brings us to the question of priorities. I was told of a man who had a very high position with a company that required him to be on the road quite often. One day, he shocked his friends in the company by giving up that position, taking a fantastic cut in salary to take a lesser position. The reason he gave was that he had taken stock of himself and discovered he was losing everything that mattered to him. His wife and children were becoming strangers to him. His church very seldom saw him. His relationship to God was dwindling away. Therefore, he gave up all of that money, for he learned that it could never buy what he needed most.

Some place in our lives, we're going to have to make that decision. Do we really have what we need for life? Are we making the best things our priority, or are the best things getting pushed aside by good things? It's easy to push aside Christ in the name of that which seems so good and so important, but which is not the best.

It's easy to choose Barabbas and leave Christ behind. Sometimes peer pressure gets us to do it. Sometimes we get angry because Christ doesn't do for us what we tell Him. Sometimes we get too busy. That is why one of the outstanding traits of the Christian is perseverance, the ability to stay with it, to keep on going in spite of what the crowd says, in spite of what life throws at you. With Christ at the center of our lives, we will not leave Him behind. We will stay close to Him.

A Jewish legend tells of the thirty-six righteous people by whose merit the world survives. The folklore of Judaism teaches that in every generation has thirty-six secret saints. Nobody knows who they are, but were it not for their solitary example the world would crumble.

A rabbi named Elie Wissel tells a story about one of these saints who came to the sinful town of Sodom, determined to save its inhabitants from destruction. Night and day he walked the streets and marketplaces of Sodom, preaching against greed and theft, falsehood and indifference. At the outset people listened and smiled condescendingly. Then they stopped listening; he no longer even amused them. The killers went on killing, and the wise kept silent, as if there were no just man in their midst.

One day a child, puzzled by the unfortunate preacher and feeling compassion for him, asked: "Poor stranger, you shout and you expend yourself body and soul. Don't you see that it is hopeless?" "Yes, I see," answered the just man. "Then why do you go on?" "I'll tell you why. In the beginning I thought I could change man. Today I know I cannot. If I still shout today and if I still scream, it is to prevent man from ultimately changing me."[6]

When the crowd yells out "Barabbas," may we have the faith and courage to cry out "Jesus!" The sound may not be loud, the voice may not sound like much, but when all is said and done, the only name that will last is the name of Jesus. Those who share that name and say it will celebrate Jesus' kingdom.

Notes

1. Gerald Freeman, "Your Sins Killed Jesus," *Quarterly Review,* Apr.-May-June 1977, p. 93.

2. Arthur Sueltz, *When the Wood is Green* (New York: Harper & Row, 1973), p. 26.

3. John Redhead, *Sermons on Bible Characters* (Nashville: Abingdon Press, 1963), p. 42.

4. Roy L. Smith, "Save Your High Moments," *Communion Meditation,* Gaston Foote, ed. (Nashville: Abingdon-Cokesbury Press, 1951), pp. 150-151.

5. Clovis Chappell, *The Sermon on the Mount* (Nashville: Abingdon-Cokesbury Press, 1930), pp. 55-56.

6. John Townsend, "Resisting the World," *The New Pulpit Digest,* May-June 1977, p. 66.

9

Simon of Cyrene: Picking Up that Cross

Mark 15:21

A young boy was listening to the teacher tell about the cross. He asked, "Could you skip this part because it's too sad. How about skipping it and get to the happy part." A middle-aged adult woman said, "I don't like to talk about the cross because it's too sad and depressing. I've got too much of that in my life already. I wish we wouldn't talk so much about the cross."

Two people, different in age and maturity, but both said the same thing. They wanted to downplay the cross in Christian experience, not talk about it so much, maybe even ignore it. They were for the happy stuff. The empty tomb that surprised the disciples, the good news of Jesus' resurrection. But they didn't want to have anything to do with the cross—that symbol of sin and shame and suffering. They'd rather leave the cross alone and not talk about it.

But Jesus talked a lot about the cross. In fact, He talked about discipleship in terms of picking up a cross. He never ignored the cross, never bypassed it. He said, "If you want to be a disciple of mine, you've got to pick up that cross." Mark 15:21 records a brief incident in the passion narrative that illustrates picking up the cross. Jesus was carrying His cross to Calvary. The cross was heavy, and He dropped it. A spectator, Simon of Cyrene, was told to pick up Jesus' cross. We don't know much about Simon. His two sons are mentioned in Scripture, maybe indicating the fact that the people to whom Mark wrote knew them. Maybe they were influential in the early church. We don't know much about Simon except that he was there and was told to pick up the cross; he was forced to do it. In that little incident is a good indication of what we are going to have to do if we're going to be the kind of disciples we need to be for Jesus Christ. We have to pick up that cross. What does that mean?

I. We Have a Choice

Jesus was carrying that heavy cross. Simon was in the crowd. Maybe he was curious about what was going on. All of a sudden, he turned from spectator to participant. A soldier made him pick up Jesus' cross. Simon was forced—compelled—to do it. But, we are not forced to take up the cross. No soldier will present the cross to us and tell us to pick it up. Instead, Jesus asks us to do it. "Here is My cross. Will you pick it up?" He does not take a hammer and bang us on the head and make us do it. He offers us the opportunity. Whether we pick up the cross is our choice.

Before we decide, we better make sure we understand what picking up that cross means, for I think we often misunderstand it. A woman with an alcoholic husband says that living with him is "bearing her cross." A fellow who is the only Christian where he works takes a lot of abuse and teasing and says that's his "cross to bear." A person with a physical handicap says that is his "cross to bear." These are terrible situations, and I wouldn't minimize them at all, but we need to understand that when Christ was talking about picking up the cross, He was not talking about bearing those burdens. The cross is a symbol of death. When Christ climbed that cross, it was a symbol of the fact that He had died to His own will. He had made that commitment to do what His Father wanted. What God wanted came first, and so He climbed the cross and died for you and me.

When we are asked to pick up the cross, we are asked to die. We are asked to die to Jesus Christ, to put our will last and God's will first. We're asked to trust Him and turn over the control of our lives to Him, to live from that day onward serving Him, loving Him, and following Him. There can be no discipleship until we die.

Once we have taken upon ourselves the will of Christ, we view life differently. Once we have died to Christ, we can deal with that alcoholic husband. Once we have died to Christ, we can deal with that situation at work. Once we have died to Christ, we can deal with that physical handicap. Once we have died to Christ, we can live a life of service and love and we can bear burdens of others. The dying comes first. We cannot live until we die.

Christ presents us that cross and says, "Will you pick it up?" Every one of us has that cross offered to us. Have we taken it? A woman who wanted to be a missionary was being interviewed for appointment. She wanted to serve in a difficult place. The committee questioning her said, "You know, you'll be lonely." She said, "I know that." "The work is hard and difficult." "I know that. I'm ready for it." "You might even be persecuted because that's an unstable country." "I know that." "You might even die." She made this statement, "I have already died. Now what I want to do is to just serve."

To take up the cross means to die to self and to live for Christ. Too many of us have not done that. We have not given ourselves up to Christ. We cannot become disciples until we take the cross offered to us.

II. We Share the Pain

When Simon picked up the cross, he shared Jesus's pain. Simon took Jesus' burden upon his back. Jesus was able to accomplish what He had to accomplish because Simon of Cyrene shared His pain.

When we assume the cross, sharing pain is part of it. When Christ took that cross, when He gave Himself to God and climbed that cross, He voluntarily took upon Himself your pain and my pain. He volunteered to share our burdens and to suffer our penalties. When we pick up the cross, we are saying that we are willing to share each other's pain. Pain is not forced upon us; we choose to take the pain, suffering, and burdens. What do you choose to put on yourself? Is there any pain, any suffering, any burden you are willing to take from somebody else's back?

A pastor in South Carolina told of a retired couple in the church who became concerned about world hunger. They had spent their lives serving Christ, and all they had in their possession was the house that they lived in. So concerned were they about world hunger that they sold their house with the provision that they could live in it until they died. They took the money they made from the sale and gave it to world hunger. They didn't have to do that. That's picking up the cross and sharing the pain.[1]

Father Damian served in a leper colony. He so cared for the lepers that he touched them. The result of his touching was that leprosy came to him. That's sharing somebody else's burden.[2] A young family, concerned about refugee children, adopted one refugee child and then two, then four, and then ten. They spent their lives caring for those nobody else seemed to care about. That's picking up the cross and sharing the pain. A woman from Union Seminary went to the ghetto to serve Christ, knowing she could be robbed and mugged and worse. But she worked to bring hope to the hopeless. That's picking up the cross and sharing the pain. A young man served as a medical missionary, turning his back on a lucrative practice here because he wanted to do something for Christ in word and deed. That's picking up the cross and sharing the pain.

How much pain have we sought to share? How many burdens have we sought to ease? How much love have we sought to give? When Christ climbed the cross, He died for us. When we pick up the cross, do we do anything for anybody else? Christ asked us to pick up the cross, and once we do, He expects us to share some of the pain and hurt in this world. He expects us to try to ease some of the pain, to stop what pain we can. How much have we willingly chosen to share?

III. We Share the Resurrection

The young boy and middle-aged woman wanted to bypass the cross, but we can't. Without the cross, there would be no resurrection; without Jesus' suffering, there would be no life. When Simon of Cyrene took up Jesus' cross, when he shared the burden that Christ had, he enabled Christ to carry out the tremendous work that He had to do. He enabled Christ to climb that hill and go through that crucifixion. When he picked up the cross, even though he didn't know it, he was helping resurrection to occur for him as well as for others.

The cross is a symbol of all that defeats us: sin, suffering, and death. Christ beat it, defeated it. An old hymn says that the way of the cross leads home. There is no other way. Through the death and resurrection of Christ—and only through that—is the way to life, life abundant, life eternal. To pick up the cross, to die to self, and live for Christ is the only way we can truly live.

During the Civil War, a company of irregulars known as bushwackers were arrested by Union soldiers. Because they were guerilla fighters and not in uniform, they were sentenced to be shot. A courageous young boy in the Union army touched his commanding officer on the arm and pleaded: "Won't you allow me to take the place of one of the men you have just condemned? I know him well; he has a large family who needs him badly. My parents are dead and I have few friends. No one will miss me. Please let me take his punishment!" The officer hesitated but finally gave his consent. Pulling the husband and father to one side, the young man filled his position on the death line. On a stone that marks his grave in a little southern town are these words: "Sacred to the Memory of Willy Lear. He took my place."[3]

Jesus did that for us. We have been rebellious, having done what we've been warned against doing. Our rebellion has put us into a debt situation. Christ has sprung our release. He has paid our debt. He died for us, and only when we identify with His death through faith can resurrection ever happen for us. Only when we pick up the cross and share it and ease the burdens of others does it help them to see that resurrection is possible for them. Only when we're ready to live the cross in our lives can the good news of it's meaning ever be seen and told in the world in which we live. Unless we take up the cross, the world dies. That's why it's important to pick it up. That's why it's important to carry it to places where we live. Only then can resurrection begin. Only then can hope begin. Only then can what Christ did come alive.

Many people want to bypass the cross. "Let's get to the happy part. Let's think of celebrations and cheers and not of agony and suffering and pain." No one likes to think of that. We're all for the good news, not the bad. But to bypass the cross is to bypass faith. There is no way to life in Christ except via Calvary and all that it means.

In the picture *Procession to Calvary* all the people are looking at Christ going up the hill. Some seemed to be bloodthirsty, all excited. Other seem to be indifferent. A child is doing a summersault, one is trying to leapfrog over a mud puddle. In the background are the two crosses on which two thieves are already hanging. In the middle of the painting is Simon of Cyrene and the Roman soldier with the cross at Simon's feet. Simon is struggling with the decision. What will he do with the cross? Will he pick it up? Does it matter? In that picture, most of the people didn't even care that the cross was there.[4]

In our day, do we care that the cross was raised on our behalf? Do we even care that it is offered to us, given to us as a chance to live? What will we do with that cross? The answer we give to that will mean life or death. May we choose wisely!

Notes

1. David Matthews, "For Her Life He Died: A Persistent Cross," *Applying the Gospel in the Local Church,* Procedings of The Christian Life Commission Seminar, Southern Baptist Convention, Ft. Worth, Tex., 1985, p. 31.

2. Keith Miller, *The Becomers* (Waco, Tex.: Word Books, 1973), p. 52.

3. Leonard Ferguson, "My Place on the Cross," *Proclaim,* Apr.-May-June 1977, p. 30.

4. John Killinger, *A Sense of His Presence* (New York: Doubleday and Co., 1977), p. 119.

10

A Tale of Two Bowls

John 13:2-5; Matthew 27:24-26

Most of us face the same choices in life. They may come in different clothing, but at the bottom, they are all about the same. The choices are between what is best and right or what is wrong, whether we will choose to accept responsibility or choose to run from it. Whether we will choose to serve the God we know as Christ or some other god we have thought to be better. Whatever decision or choice we make, those factors are usually involved.

Often the success or failure of life for us depends on the answers we give. The reason some live life to the fullest and some are fed up with it comes from the answers to the questions. Which choices will we make? The experiences of two men during passion week reflect choices made. This is the tale of two bowls.

The first man to be considered is Jesus. He was in the upper room facing the cross. He knew it was coming, and He was frightened. He wanted to share a moment with His disciples. He needed to, but the disciples were arguing among themselves over who was the greatest disciple among them. On the table lay a bowl and a towel. Usually a servant washed the guests' feet when they entered a home. On that night, nobody had washed the guests' feet when they had arrived. None of the disciples were going to humble themself enough to wash anybody else's feet. Jesus reached for the towel and the basin, got down on His hands and knees, and began to wash the disciples' dirty feet.

The other man is Pilate. Pilate was faced with a choice: to set Jesus free or to crucify Him. Pilate turned Jesus over to the soldiers and religious leaders to be crucified. When he did so, he brought a bowl and washed his hands in it and said, "It's not my fault."

Two men faced difficult decisions. Would each make a wrong decision or a right decision? What entered into their decision making, and what enters into the decisions we make?

I. Self-Sacrifice or Self-Service?

Jesus and Pilate could have made other choices and saved their own necks. Jesus was tempted to. Remember, the cross was a frightening experience to Him. He didn't have to take it. He could choose. In the garden of Gethsemane, He prayed for another way. He was faced with the cross. Would He take it? Would He pass it by? Would He save His own neck, or would He climb the cross to serve other people? Would He do what was right, responsible, and godly, or would He turn away?

Pilate had the same choice. Pilate knew that Jesus was innocent. Jesus hadn't done anything wrong. Pilate seems to have wanted to set Him free, but he had many things to consider. The Jewish leaders were upset, and Pilate didn't want them to be upset. He had to keep the peace, for his Roman superiors didn't want any trouble in the province. Already Pilate had had troubles and had been warned to keep the peace. Also, Pilate enjoyed his position of wealth and power. He had a choice to make. He knew Jesus was innocent. What would he do? Would he serve himself, or would he do what was right and responsible and godly?

We know the outcome. Jesus said yes to others and climbed the cross and became the means through which people could find hope. Pilate said yes to himself and saved his own neck, for a while. Soon he lost his position and his power. One said yes to God and found life. One said yes to himself and lost what he had hoped to keep.

We have to make our decisions too. The choices may not seem as radical as those Jesus and Pilate had to make, but we do have to decide whether we will serve ourselves or God and others.

How do we make career choices? Do we decide on the basis of what we can get out of it for ourselves or how we can use our work to serve humanity and better the world? Which way do we look upon our work and our career? A man felt he was being called to be a missionary, but he also had an opportunity to be a computer programmer. As a computer programmer, he would have a higher salary and easier working conditions than he would have as a missionary in some far country. He had to make the decision. What would he do? He left a fifty-thousand-dollar-a-year job to go back to seminary to study to be a minister. When people asked him how he could do it, he said simply, "Because I discovered that earning fifty thousand dollars a year did not bring me what I needed." How do we decide our work? Self-sacrifice or self service?

How do we make decisions about popularity? We all struggle with wanting to be popular. We are faced every now and then with decisions to drink or not to drink, to take drugs or not to take drugs, to be sexually free or sexually responsible, to go to church or not to go to church. These decisions ask us what price will we pay to be popular, to be one of the group? Will we go along because that's what's best for us, or will we turn away because it's not best for us or for others?

How do we decide about our involvement in church or other moral issues? To tithe or not to tithe, what is the right decision to make there? To be involved in the many ministries of the church, to sing, to teach, to serve on committees, or to visit—which one is right? And as a disciple, will we be honest when others are cheating? Will we be faithful to our marriage vows when others say it's all right not to be? Will we cheat on exams since everyone else does? What will we do? We are faced always with decisions, and the question is: Will we serve ourselves or serve God? These are not easy decisions to make. We always need to ask ourselves: What is right? What is responsible? What is godly?

Some years ago a great fire burned the Iroquois Theater in Chicago. Over five hundred people were burned and trampled to death in the panic. Two college students were attending the program that afternoon. When the fire started, they both rushed for the door and got out. One student went across the street to a building, went up to the second floor, got a big, large wooden plank, and put it in one of the windows of the Iroquois Theater. He carried twenty-three people to safety. He was burned severely. The other student ran. Something happened to him after that. He seemed to have lost control of himself; and everywhere he went, he would say, "Do you know me? I was in the Iroquois Theater fire, but I saved myself." Years later the same man was going up to people saying, "Do you know me? I was in the Iroquois Theater fire, but I saved myself."[1] The guilt of that, how heavy a burden it was to carry! Would we have saved ourselves and forgotten others?

A lot of theological truths can be found in the comic strip *Peanuts*. One day Lucy and Linus had a chicken wishbone and were going to pull it to make a wish. Lucy was explaining to Linus that if he got the bigger half of it his wish would come true. Linus said to her, "Do I have to say the wish out loud?" Lucy said, "Of course, if you don't say it out loud it won't come true." So Lucy went ahead and made her wishes first. She said, "I wish for four new sweaters, a new bike, a new pair of skates, a new dress and one hundred dollars." It came time for Linus to make his wishes, and he said, "I wish for a long life for all of my friends, I wish for world peace, I wish for great advancements in medical research." About that time, Lucy took the wishbone and threw it away and said, "Linus, that's the trouble with you, you're always spoiling everything."[2]

Jesus said, "He who finds his life will lose it, and he who loses his life for my sake will find it" (Matt. 10:39). In all of the decisions we make, this is the part to consider. Are we serving others and serving God or are we serving ourselves?

II. Courage or Cowardice

Jesus reached a crisis point where a decision had to be made. Would He obey God or save Himself? Would He accept the responsibility or run from it? Jesus wrestled with those questions. The cross was a frightening thing to behold. It meant death, pain, and suffering. For a moment, He withdrew from it, frightened by it. But He said, "Nevertheless not my will, but thine, be done" (Luke 22:42). He chose to climb the cross. He chose to be the Servant. Courage took Jesus to the cross, courage kept Him there through the pain and the suffering, and courage carried Him through. He had the courage to do what was right, the courage to do what was responsible, the courage to do what God wanted.

Pilate also faced a crisis. He wanted to please the Jewish leaders; he wanted to keep the peace in his own province. He wanted to keep his power. At the same time, he knew that Jesus was innocent and that he would be condemning an innocent man to death. Pilate had the power to set Jesus free; but when the decision had to be made, Pilate did not have the courage to do what was right and best. He called for a basin and washed his hands to tell everybody he was not responsible for the consequences of his decision. What a joke! What a laugh! No matter how many times Pilate washed his hands, he would never be able to wash the guilt away. It would still be there, haunting him all the days of his life. He didn't do what was right and responsible. He lacked the courage.

I wonder if we'll have courage to stand for our convictions. It will not be easy. There will be pain to suffer and risks to run.

Do we have the courage of our convictions in the area of race relations? We know that God created everyone in His image, that God is no respecter of persons. That means we should treat everyone as a child of God, regardless of race and color of skin. But do we do it? In Tennessee some years ago, a pastor tried to stand up for the betterment of all races. He supported the desegregation of schools in his community, and he was beaten up for that by members of his own church. I ask you, who had the courage, who were the cowards? We have to make that same decision even now. In our time, are we treating people equally, or trying to? Are we really concerned about the quality of opportunity for all people? Do we decide the issues on the basis of what is best for all or what is best for us? To make a decision and to stand in behalf of it requires courage. Will we have it?

Do we have the courage of our convictions about world peace? This is one of the hotly contested issues of our time and, in my opinion, one of the most important issues. How do we stand? We know God is against war. We know God doesn't want people killing one another. How do we stop it? How do we become peacemakers? Many stand up and say, "Let's have a nuclear freeze and move toward nuclear disarmament." They are frequently accused of being unpatriotic, Communist, unrealistic, fools. Others stand and call for an escalation of the arms race. They run the risk of bringing the world closer to a nuclear war. Which side is right? How do we stand?

Will you have the courage of your convictions, whatever they are? Will you have the courage to do right when everyone else is doing wrong? When all are saying yes, will you have the courage to say no. Even in your personal frustrations—when you've lost a job or you've lost a loved one or you're sick or you're heartbroken—will you have the courage to face up to that? Or will you pine away in self-pity, bemoaning all the terrible things that life has done to you? Will you stand up and knock on door after door after door until you find a job? Will you stand up and keep on going in the face of death because you know that is what you must do? Will you, if you cannot overcome your sickness, learn not to let it conquer your spirit? Or if heartbroken, will you learn to take the risk again of love, knowing that is the only way you'll ever find it?

Living this Christian life calls for courage, moral courage, to stand up for what is right and responsible and godly, moral courage to do the right thing at the right time and in the right spirit. In our day, we don't need those who will not have the courage and the backbone to stand up.

Harper Lee wrote the beautiful story *To Kill a Mockingbird*. Atticus Finch was a lawyer in a small Southern town. One day he was called upon to defend a young black man who had been charged with attacking a white girl. When he agreed to defend the young man, he immediately came under the abuse, the scorn, of the people in the town. The boy was innocent, and Atticus Finch defended him capably; but when the jury came in, nobody was surprised that its verdict was *guilty*. Atticus Finch's two children were at the courthouse. Unable to find seats downstairs, they had gone into the segregated balcony and had sat next to the town's black preacher. As the judge retired and the spectators filed out of the courtroom, Jean, Atticus's daughter, was engrossed in watching her father. He stood alone in the room, placing papers from the table into his briefcase. He put on his coat and walked down the middle aisle toward the exit—a beaten man but with soul intact. Jean felt someone touch her shoulder. She turned around and noticed that everyone in the balcony was standing. The black preacher nudged her again and said, "Miss Jean, stand up, your father is passing by."[3]

I wonder, Will anybody ever stand up when we pass by because we have sought to do the right thing regardless of the consequences, because we have sought to do the godly thing regardless of the price? Will we have the courage to stand up and do what needs to be done?

Two bowls: they are offered to us all. One bowl Christ took, and it led to a cross but then to life. One bowl Pilate took, and it led away from the cross and then to death. They had to choose which bowl they would take.

So do we! Will it be self-sacrifice or self-service? Will it be courage or cowardice? Will it be the way of Christ or the way of Pilate? Our answer will lead us to life or death. Please, choose well!

Notes

1. Joseph Sizoo, *Still We Can Hope* (Nashville: Abingdon Press, 1966), pp. 109-110.

2. Roland Perdue, "Well, Somebody's Got to Make Mousetraps!" *Master Sermons,* Dec. 1979, pp. 612-612.

3. *Pulpit Resource,* July-Aug.-Sept. 1979, p. 13.

Series III

Easter Sermons

Each of these sermons seeks to give a slightly different approach to presenting the Easter message. It is hard to avoid some repetition since the eternal truth of Easter is always the same. These sermons may provide some help in understanding how to preach the Easter story.

Sermons

11

Ringing the Rusty Bells of Hope
Matthew 28:1-10

Once I remember seeing an old church in the country. The church had once been the center of a thriving community. But the community had died, and the church died with it. The church stood still and quiet, gathering dust and cobwebs. In the front churchyard was the bell that had called people to church, the bell that had reminded the people of the church and of the presence of God among them, the bell that kept alive their hope. But it was caked with rust and was still and quiet, never ringing out any word of hope because there was no one to ring it.

Some people today say we are in a hopeless situation, with nothing to ring any bells about. Around the world, we see war; trouble between black and white, white and red, and more; poverty and hunger and sickness and disease. We also have our personal problems: loneliness, boredom, misery, and unhappiness. In the midst of all of that, the church announces, "Christ is alive!" and the world turns and says, "So what?"

Well, so what? What difference does it make that Christ is alive? How has Christ's resurrection changed our lives? Can we ring the rusty bells of hope again? Does Easter mean that?

Tom Dooley, the missionary doctor who spent his life in service to the people of Indochina and who died at a young age with cancer, wrote of a time when he was discouraged. Money wasn't coming in; supplies were too few; work was hard and tedious. He wrote, "Everytime I get discouraged and down in the dumps someone comes along and rings the rusty bells of hope and I have encouragement to get back at it again."[1] I think that's a very powerful phrase, "ringing the rusty bells of hope," for that is what Easter is all about. At Easter God once again rings the bells of hope, announcing to the world that He is alive and real and available, announcing that we can always have hope because there is always God.

The disciples needed to hear the Easter message of hope because they

95

had lost hope. They had put their faith in Christ; but after Christ's death, they seemed to have no faith left. They didn't know what was going to become of them. After the resurrection, they changed completely. The disciples united to change the world. They had heard the rusty bells of hope. What we need to do is to discover just what Easter means to us so that *we* can ring our bells loud and clear.

I. A Purpose Worth Living and Dying For

All of the disciples had jobs and professions, families and friends. They left that behind because they thought they had found in Christ something greater than all that. They had found a cause and a purpose worth everything they had to give. Christ was up to something good and great. Christ's words and deeds seemed to confirm that. He was a man who was going to change the world, and they left everything to follow Him. Then, the crucifixion! They didn't know what was going to happen to them. What were they going to do? They scattered into the night, as people without purpose usually do. Then came the resurrection, and they got back together and started to preach and serve once more. They had learned that the cause Christ had set out to accomplish would be accomplished. Not even the ugly crucifixion could keep Christ from accomplishing His purpose. Christ could not be defeated.

One of today's problems is lack of purpose. We don't know what we're here to do. We can't find our place in the sun. We are restless and miserable because we just don't know what life is all about. We're trying to find a place to go, but we're not too sure there *is* any place to go.

Loren Eisley wrote of the time when he rode on a train at midnight. He went into the smoking room, and there, in the middle of the room, was what he described as a bum: unshaven, disheveled clothes, eyes blank as if they were staring into nothingness, a brown bag on his lap that seemed to contain everything he possessed. The conductor came in saying, "Tickets please." All eyes were focused on that man, for they thought that he didn't have a ticket. The man reached down into his old, battered coat pocket and pulled out a big wad of bills; he handed them to the conductor and said, "Give me a ticket to . . ." and he paused a moment, "Give me a ticket to wherever it is."[2]

Where are you going? Often we're looking for a cause that will survive, so we try anything, not knowing where we're going. We try drugs and alcohol; we try the satanic and the occult; we try this and that, anything that will bring us purpose, a meaning worth living and dying for. However, we never seem to find it. The causes and people we latch onto seem to be so temporary.

But Christ comes to say one cause will conquer and is worth living and dying for. It's the cause of building up humanity by building up the kingdom of God. It's not easy. It's a challenge; it's an adventure. It's hard to try to bring peace. It's hard to try to do away with injustice. It's hard to feed the hungry and visit the sick. It's hard to try to build up humanity. It will take a lifetime plus. We can spend our lives doing it, and we'll never be able to see the end of it. But Christ promises us that every word we speak in this work, every deed we do in this work will last. The truth of the resurrection is that the kingdom of Christ is the kingdom that will last forever and ever. Anyone who puts self into that kingdom has become part of a cause that won't die.

Two friends graduated from college. One became a business executive, and one went to spend his life working in the ghetto with the under-privileged. One day the business executive, who worked in a defense plant and became rich and wealthy, visited his friend and said, "I don't understand it. You have a college education; you could have done exactly what I did. You could have become a successful business executive and built a kingdom for yourself. Instead, you spend your life down here in the ghetto trying to help these underprivileged people; I don't under-stand it." The other man said, "Well, I guess the reason I do it is somehow I feel that what I am doing will have more lasting effect in the long run than what you are doing." What are we doing? When we die, will the world care that we have ever been? Or will we leave something done for God that will have permanent significance? The kingdom of Christ is forever and ever, and so are those who are in it.

II. We Are Not Alone

The crucifixion was a tragedy to the disciples. They didn't know what to do. They didn't know how to handle Christ's death. It knocked them for a loop. They had depended on Christ for everything, but now He was gone. They felt abandoned, alone. But it wasn't so! Christ rose to tell them that, in the midst of all of their problems, they were not alone because He was alive. He would be the source of their strength. The disciples believed Christ, and they went out into a world that didn't particularly want them. They went out to endure prison cells and dun-geons and death. They went out to do witness, confident that as they lived Christ would live with them.

All of us sometimes get some tough experiences from life. There's no doubt about this, we may just as well admit it. Life presents us with difficulties and problems. The problem often is that we have tried to solve problems by ourselves. We have swallowed the philosophy of individualism which says, "Do your own thing; do what you want to do; you don't need anybody else." So we sing that spiritual which says, "I must face that lonesome valley,/I must face it for myself,/nobody else can face it for me,/I must face it for myself." We try valiantly to stand up to life and declare, "We'll conquer you; we'll do what we want to do," and life smiles its silly grin and says, "Oh?" Then it knocks us down again and again. We have tried to live life too much on our own and have been blinded to the fact that help is available. The resurrection means that the power of Christ is available for us now, that Christ is not dead but living. He comes to dwell within us in the Holy Spirit to give that which we need, to give the courage to go one more step, to give the strength to endure what we didn't think we could endure, and to help through the dark nights. Christ does not come in life to help us around our crosses or over our crosses, but Christ comes to help us bear our crosses and turn them into victories. Christ comes to say that we are not alone, ever.

Wiley Rutledge, a preacher in Tennessee, told of an experience he had with his young son. Rutledge, his wife, and their son were driving late at night, and his son was in the back seat all alone. The boy asked his father, "Is it true what you say, that God is everywhere?" "Yes, Son, it's true." "Does that mean God is here in the backseat with me?" "Yes, Son, wherever you are, God is. He's there in the backseat with you." Rutledge thought he'd answered his son pretty well. After a moment or two of silence, a trembling voice said, "I know God is back here with me, but could I climb up front with you and Mama?"

We've heard it before, "Yes, God is with us in the dark," but we're still afraid. We haven't learned that Christ comes to live with us and help us face the dark. In all of life's experiences, whatever we have to deal with, in the midst of them is a Presence who wants to help us. If the resurrection means anything, it means Christ is with us now. We are not alone!

III. Life Beyond the Physical

The disciples thought when Christ was crucified that was the end! They had heard Christ talk about the resurrection, but they never understood it. When Christ was crucified, they didn't know what to do. They were confused and bewildered and lost. They thought death was the end. But Christ came to prove it wasn't so. The disciples were as surprised as anyone that Christ rose from the dead. They had not expected it, and they had a hard time believing it. Finally, they believed that life was more than just physical or more than what one could just see and feel, that there was another dimension to life which could not be killed. There was more beyond!

One question which we must answer someplace, sometime, is, Is life basically physical, is it only that which we can see and touch and feel? Is there some dimension in which dwells love and hope and truth and beauty and goodness? Is there a part of life that does not die? Are we more than flesh and bones? If we say life is more than physical, we must answer the next question: What is that more, and where is that more going to end?

Without belief in the God of purpose and love, only one answer can be given: We're going nowhere. Life for us is an accident; at death that accident will be corrected, and we will be erased from the face of time. If that's what you want to believe, believe it. But I cannot. I cannot believe that the goodness and beauty and joy that we experience with each other is an accident and stops at death. Neither did the disciples. They were cowards, but something changed them. They were concerned about their physical safety when Christ was crucified; but after the resurrection, they cared little about it. They faced all kinds of dangers and even death, little concerned about their physical safety because they had found something more important. They had found a spiritual security that was more valuable than life itself. They had found that life could not be torn from the hands of God.

To be honest, we don't believe that too much in twentieth-century America. We have learned well the lessons that science and technology have taught us: believe only in the facts, only in those things you can prove. However, not much in life can be proved beyond a shadow of a doubt. Some of the best things in life cannot be proved by test tube or analysis. Take love, for instance. We know that love is. How do we test it? How do we see it? How do we know what it is? Can we put it in a laboratory? We can't even define it. All we can do is see the results of love—the looks, the touches, the tenderness,—we know that love is.

The same is true of the resurrection. We cannot prove it, but we can see the results of it, and that makes it more probable to believe. We see that cowardly disciples became courageous. We can see a church nurtured down through two thousand years, not as a monument to a dead person (those kinds of institutions usually fade into museums) but as a fellowship of a *living* Christ. We feel within ourselves that there is more beyond. We cannot be satisfied with the cold fact that death is the end.

However, while we can gather ideas to make the belief in the resurrection more probable; when we get down to it, the resurrection is a matter of faith. We have to take a jump, take a chance. Since we can believe the disciples and since we can believe what Christ said, then there is no doubt that there is life beyond. There is more than the physical.

Cecil deMille, the Hollywood producer, was resting in a canoe one day, when a big black beetle jumped up on the canoe and sat there. It fascinated deMille, and he looked down and saw that many of its relatives were still swimming in the lake, mired in the mud. He thought, *It's a shame that those beetles in the bottom of the lake can't know the world that this beetle up on the canoe is knowing.* After a while, the heat of the sun was too much for the beetle, and it was killed. Then something amazing occurred: the shell of that beetle split down the back, and another mass came out of it, a mass which opened itself up with four wings that had glorious colors. That beetle had become a dragon fly. Cecil deMille had witnessed a metamorphosis. The dragon fly left his shell behind and went out into the sky to his new world. DeMille said, "If the Creator can provide that much for a lowly beetle, what does He have in store for man?"[3]

The resurrection says we don't really know, but one thing is certain: Christ is in store for believers and where Christ is, is enough. We must live by faith that one day we will go home to His kingdom.

Too often we have let the bells be silent; we have not rung them loud and clear. We have not been sure ourselves whether there's any reason to ring them. If Easter means anything to us, it means that there is a purpose and a life that cannot be conquered. We who attach ourselves to that purpose are on the right track. It means that in the midst of our helping to bring in the kingdom there is a Presence with us, a Christ who resides not out there only but with us here, helping us face life. It means that He will do this not only here but forever, and forever is a long, long time.

A belief in the resurrection is not ours just because a book in the Bible says there was an empty tomb. We believe in the resurrection because we have experienced the truth of the Bible in that someplace, sometime, somewhere, that strange, mysterious Presence of God came to us. For a moment, at least, we knew He was alive with us. If that has happened to you once, it ought to be enough to cause your life always to ring the rusty bells of hope.

Mrs. Mulvaney was a Red Cross worker when she and 4,000 others were captured by the Japanese in 1942. They were put into a prison camp that accommodated 450. There were hardships—overcrowding, loneliness, isolation, and suffering. The people felt like all had forgotten them, even God. On that first Easter Sunday, Mrs. Mulvaney—on behalf of the others—went to the Japanese commandant and asked permission to sing some hymns. "Why?" he asked. "Because Christ rose from the dead," she replied. "No!" Twelve times this ritual of request and refusal was acted out. Finally, the word came that all the women in their prison camp would be allowed to sing praises to God for five minutes in courtyard one. They were led out and, under the watchful eye of one guard, sang praises to God for five minutes, thanking Him for His resurrection, and for hope. When the singing was over and they were being led back into their places, Mrs. Mulvaney was stopped by that Japanese guard. He reached into his brown shirt and took out a tiny orchid. He placed it in her hand and leaned over to her and whispered, "Christ *did* rise." He did an about-face and was gone, and Mrs. Mulvaney stood there crying because she knew that not only did Christ rise but that He had been seen and known.[4]

Christ is alive! Do you see; do you know? It's true! Christ is risen! Hallelujah! Ring those bells!

Notes

1. Clarence J. Forsberg, "The Day That Hope Was Born," *Pulpit Preaching,* Feb. 1971, pp. 18-19.

2. Ernest Campbell, "Because He Came," *Sermons From Riverside,* 24 Dec. 1972, p. 2.

3. Leonard Griffith, *God's Time and Ours* (New York: Abingdon Press, 1964), p. 103.

4. Ibid., pp. 116-117.

12

The Gifts Easter Brings

Matthew 28:1-10

After last Easter, I heard some kids in the neighborhood talking, and one of them asked the other, "What did you get for Easter?" He mentioned all sorts of things: Easter eggs, chocolate bunnies, clothes, and such. That surprised me. I could understand things for Christmas but getting something for Easter, the celebration of the resurrection of Christ? Then I began to remember that we've commercialized Easter just like other religious days. For many, Easter will be just a time for bunny rabbits, jelly beans, bonnets, and parades. That's all there is. What did you get for Easter? Something material, and that's it?

Somehow we don't feel that is right. There has to be more to it than that. More people come to church on Easter than on any other Sunday of the year. Why do we come? Because we're always looking for something to remind us that our lives are not in vain. We still cling to the hope, however vague at times, that God is and He cares what happens to us, that God lives among us and is able to help us with all of our problems, even the problem of death.

We are living in difficult times. War could break out in the Middle East. Africa is experiencing revolts. South America is in chaos. Hunger and starvation exist across the face of the earth. Racial unrest, violence, and corruption spread in our own land. Add to that all our personal troubles—sickness and suffering, disappointment and defeat, and death. We wonder, in the face of these tremendous problems, is there any word from God? Is there any hope? Is there something we can find to help us live life and live it triumphantly?

Easter holds the answers to those questions. We *do* get something for Easter—not material gifts but spiritual gifts from God through Christ. Easter brings us the key to living. The disciples did not live in good times either. Christ had been crucified. Their hope had been demolished. Life for them was darkness. When the women went to the tomb, they were going to anoint a dead body. All of a sudden, the truth broke forth: "He is not here; for he has risen" (v. 6). The resurrection made a tremendous difference in the lives of the disciples. From that moment on, they went out to live abundantly, hopefully, eternally. They received at Easter what God had to give. What does Easter bring to us that can help us live triumphantly?

I. A New perspective About Life

Despair marked the faces of the disciples after the crucifixion. Their hope had been crucified. They had believed in Jesus. They thought He was going to bring in the Kingdom, and they wanted to be a part of that kingdom. They had heard Jesus' teachings and had seen His tremendous deeds and His miracles. The world needed a man like Him. They had left much to follow Him: jobs, families, and friends. They put their lives in His hands, and now He was dead! In the face of death, He didn't try to do a thing to overcome it. The disciples only knew darkness. It covered the face of their earth.

The disciples went to the tomb and heard the words, "He is not here; for he has risen"! They began to realize that the crucifixion was not the last word about Christ. There was a word about Him on Sunday. The resurrection swallowed up the crucifixion; light overcame darkness. They began to take a new look at life and see it from a different perspective. They realized that life was under the control of God, and that, even though things got dark and difficult, it was not the final word. Life was in God's hands. Final defeat and final tragedy did not exist. Crucifixion was followed by resurrection. They went out to change the world. It wasn't easy for them. They were disappointed. They faced dangers all the time. They faced death constantly. I'm sure there must have been times when they said, "Things look bad. We're not getting anywhere. Nobody seems to want to hear us. But let's not quit. Let's wait and see what tomorrow brings." With this conviction that light always follows darkness, they were able to plod their way across the face of this earth and change it.

As we think about the problems of today and our own personal difficulties, we may become pessimists. It's easy to throw up our hands in despair. Life *is* difficult. Issac Singer, a Jewish playwright, wrote his first play at sixty-nine years of age. It was entitled: *The Miracle*. The point of it was that because we are so bored with life we turn to wickedness, but that doesn't satisfy either. There's boredom and wickedness and nothing else. Issac Singer was a pessimist. He didn't believe life really means much. In an interview, he pointed out that he once believed in social justice and believed that people ought to work for it. He didn't any longer. The reason he didn't work for social justice was because he felt it wouldn't do any good. There's always wrong, there's always injustice. It just doesn't do any good to work for it. He said, "I have given up."[1]

Do we ever feel like giving up? As we look around at the problems of our day, as we try to make our way through life, how difficult it gets. The problems seem immense. The pain seems unbearable. The darkness is too dark. We begin to feel that life isn't worth living. Suicides are rising today, especially among the young. Many have decided that life isn't worth living.

Easter reminds us that we need to enlarge our vision of life. A fly lands on one of Raphael's masterpieces. Where the fly is, it's not a very good view. The texture of the painting is rough, it is difficult, and the fly doesn't understand it. The colors are all meshed together, and it doesn't make sense to the fly. From the viewpoint of the fly, it's ugliness. The fly needs to get away from the picture and see it in it's totality before it will make sense. Likewise, before we pass judgment on how life is, we've got to wait until we get a full view. Since a full view is God's view, we can say that crucifixions are followed by resurrections. Unrighteousness will be overcome by righteousness. Evil will ultimately be conquered by good.

When we want to throw up our hands in despair as we face our own personal darkness, we need to look at God's view of life. One day we will discover light that no darkness can overcome.

II. A New Sensitivity and Awareness of Life

After the crucifixion, life no longer held any sense of joy and anticipation for the disciples. Life became something to be endured, not enjoyed. It was long and hard and tedious. They didn't expect anything out of it. They made plans to go back to the dull routine of life. That's all there was. Then Mary went to the tomb to anoint a dead Christ, and she heard Jesus say, "Mary!" Suddenly, she discovered that He was alive! She was overcome by joy. Two disciples walked down the Emmaus road, talking about the crucifixion. A stranger appeared with them and interpreted Scripture for them. After a while they sat down to eat and discovered: "It is Him!" They ran back to Jerusalem to tell the others. "We have seen Him! He is alive!" Life changed for them at that moment. No longer was it something to be endured: life was something to be enjoyed! Where would He turn up next? Who would He see next? What would happen next? They didn't know, but they became alive spiritually. They were on their tiptoes because at any moment, in any person, in any event, Christ might come crashing into their lives and overcome them with joy and happiness.

Life is not something to be endured. It is to be celebrated. It is the arena where Christ is. Unfortunately, some of us do not have that sensitivity toward life. Most of us are bored with life. For most of us, it's a routine matter, no anticipation, no excitement about living.

We had an Easter egg hunt for our children in the front yard. Anticipation and excitement overcame them. Every tree, every bush, every corner of that front yard became alive for them because they might find some treasure. Often during the year, the children had passed those trees and bushes and never even noticed them. They didn't matter to them then. Now it was all different. The children were sensitive to everything in the front yard.

What would happen to us if we started living life with that kind of anticipation and excitement? If we began to realize that every event we share in, every deed we do, in every person we meet, we might discover that Christ is with us?

The magazine article entitled, "The Day That Changed a Life," was the story of a young office worker who changed the atmosphere of the place where she worked. Her attitude was so different that everyone was changed by it. Her employer asked, "What's the difference?" She replied:

> I wasn't enjoying life. It was boring to me. I was down and depressed. In the midst of it, I made up my mind to do one thing. I would try to live one day of my life as if God was really with me. I believed it. I had said the words, but I never really lived them. I would try it in what I did, in the conversations I shared. You know something? I discovered life. I tried to do it a second day, and a third day, and it go to the place where life was exciting for me because He was there. I knew Christ by words. Now I *know* Him by experience.[2]

What changes would occur in your life if you tried that? What would happen if you opened your life up to Christ; to realize that He is in your home, in all the relationships you share with your family? What if you realized that He is in your work and in the way you do it; that He is in your play; that He is with you as you celebrate life and the beauty and joy of it? The resurrection message is simple. Christ is here and, because He is, we can wake up to life and not just pass it by.

III. A New Dynamic for Living

The disciples on that Friday were just a useless bunch of men. They had really let Christ down. When He needed them, they turned away. When He was taken prisoner, they ran. When He was crucified, they hid. They disappointed Him. They misunderstood Him. They denied Him. I'm sure we would have understood if Christ had written them off as a bad investment.

However, Christ's judgment was different from ours; he believed in them. After the resurrection, the disciples did not let Him down. They spread the resurrection story across the earth. Under God's inspiration, they wrote our Scriptures. They established our churches. They kept the faith. They suffered, and most of them died violent deaths, but never again did they run away. Never again did they hide in fear. What made the difference? They had discovered that Easter was true, that Christ was with them. Since He was with them, they could meet whatever they had to meet. He was not a distant memory; He was a vital force. They did not waver.

This is an Easter truth we need to understand: Christ is alive, and He is alive for a purpose. That purpose is to bring us abundant life, and He wants to work among us to bring to this world His kingdom and to make of us, new persons. He wants us to turn our crucifixion into resurrection. He does not come to take us away from our problems. He does not come to help us forget our problems or run away from our problems. He comes to help us wrestle with our problems and triumph over them. He can do it! Christ will work in our lives. We don't always understand how, but He is the power that helps us to see our problems through when we don't think we can, to go through one more dark night when we don't think we can make it, to take one more step when we're too tired to go any further. The power of Christ is a power available today to help us to live through whatever we must.

Gary Hylton, thirty-year-old golf pro of the Lynchburg Golf Club, died of cancer. I just passed over the article about Hylton's death, thinking, *That's sad.* The next day my friend David Henry, a fellow pastor, told me that Gary had been a member of his church when he had served in Lynchburg. He shared an article with me that had been written by Bill Smith, sportswriter for the Charleston, West Virginia Mail. Smith had met Gary and was impressed by Gary's tremendous courage. Since high school, Gary had undergone fifty-one operations. His left leg was removed, part of his right arm was removed, and part of his right jaw was removed. He had cancer in his chest, in his rib cage, and all over. He walked with a limp from chemotherapy and radiology treatments. He had become addicted to drugs, and had gone through withdrawal in order to conquer that problem. Pain was a constant companion. But there he was, a pro at a golf club, playing golf with one hand, enjoying, laughing, celebrating life.

Smith asked Gary about his lonely fight with cancer. Gary Hylton said:

> "I'm nobody special. I'm just a young man who has cancer and I'm trying to live one day at a time, and every day is beautiful. Don't get the idea that I'm full of courage. I went through periods of tremendous self-pity. I fell on my knees and sobbed like a baby and asked God, 'Why me?' I was in such pain that I wasn't worried about dying. I was afraid I was going to live. There is physical courage and mental courage. I've been both routes. The mental part is the toughest. Besides, I've seen so many people worse off than me."

He went to play golf with laughter. And Bill Smith added, "I believe God gives special courage to special people. Gary Hylton was a special person."[3]

As I read about Gary's life, I wondered how he could stand the pain? How could he overcome his emotional anguish and self-pity? How could he get to the place that he celebrated life in spite of his difficulties? The answer is that the grace of God is able to help us in the midst of all of our problems. He can help us through.

One of the privileges of being a pastor is sharing in the lives of those who have found God's grace to be sufficient. I have seen believers overcome with grief make their way through that terrible valley of the shadow of death to God. I have seen believers whose hearts have been broken and whose homes have fallen apart courageously keep going, trying to make something better out of a tragic situation. I have seen many believers, who have been knocked down by life's cruelties, pick up the pieces of their lives and put them back together again. I have seen God's grace abounding often enough to say to you that it is real. Whatever difficulty we face, whatever struggle we have, wherever we have to go,

Christ can help us. The resurrected Christ is not just a song we sing or words we say: He is a power we experience. He is able!

What do we get for Easter? We get life and a chance to live forever. We get a new perspective on life as Christ reminds us that no matter how dark the darkness, He is light. We get a new sensitivity to life; life is to be enjoyed, not endured. We get a new dynamic for living; whatever we have to face, we can face it with Christ's help. These are the gifts that God has brought us in Christ. But like all gifts they must be received or they are in vain. Simply hearing and singing about God's gifts to us in Christ does not make them ours. We must commit ourselves to God through Christ and receive our gifts.

A shepherd remembered an angel saying, "Follow the star. The babe is born in Bethlehem." Years later he told his grandson all that the angel had said. The boy asked, "Well, was it true? Was He born? Was it true?" The shepherd sadly answered, "I don't know. I never took the trouble to go and see."[4]

The danger of Easter is that we will hear the cry, "He has risen!" but we will not take the trouble to see if it is true. We will not come to the place where we commit our lives to the Christ who is alive. We must make a serious commitment to Him. Once we make that commitment, every day we live will be Easter.

Notes

1. John W. Morrow, "The New Pessimism," *Master Sermons,* Jan. 1974, p. 32.

2. Leonard Griffith, *Barriers to Christian Belief* (New York: Harper & Row, 1961), p. 190.

3. Bill Smith, "Hylton: Courageous Young Man," *The News,* Lynchburg, Virginia, Sunday, 1 June 1975, Section B, p. 4.

4. Taylor Roth, "Surprised By Life," *Pulpit,* Mar. 1959, pp. 21-24.

13

The Song of Easter

John 19:41

In the geographical center of Florida, the Bok Tower rises 205 feet. It is surrounded by landscaped gardens on 53 acres. At the entrance to the tower by the wrought-iron gate, is a white slab of marble. It is Henry Bok's tomb. That tower is a tomb. It is hard to imagine that because the beauty of the flowers and of the landscaped grounds and the chimes ringing from the tower continuously remind one of life, not of death; of beauty, not despair![1]

The resurrection song is about life. John, in his Gospel, gave us this insight. The tomb where they laid Christ was in "a garden" (19:41). The tomb was in a place of life, not death. Christ is hope and joy and living, not sorrow and sadness and despair. The song of Easter is a hallelujah chorus, not a funeral dirge. He has risen! He is alive! Christ rose from the dead! That is what Easter celebrates.

I wish I could prove to you that Easter is true. I wish I could sit down and give you reasons that would help you believe that the resurrection is a fact. Belief in it is an act of faith. We must come to the place where we accept it as true and live in the light of it.

Most of us worshiping today do believe in the resurrection. We are here, not to argue about the resurrection, but to celebrate it. What does living in the light of the resurrection mean? What does saying that Christ is alive mean for us? What song does Easter give us to sing, regardless of our circumstances, regardless of our conditions? John Redhead, former pastor of The First Presbyterian Church of Greensboro, North Carolina, had some good insight at this point. He suggested the song of Easter can be written in three verses.

I. Goodness and Right Are the Victors

Before resurrection Sunday, the disciples had no song of joy to sing, only songs of mourning. Their tunes were written in the minor keys of sorrow and sadness and despair. Christ was dead, and everything worth singing about had died with Him. Wrong seemed to have conquered good, evil seemed to have conquered righteousness, hate seemed to have conquered love on the cross. The disciples couldn't understand it. They had begun to believe that life made sense, that it had meaning to it, that tomorrow had some promise. But now, no more! On the cross, death conquered life. That was it! There was no more to be said. The disciples were filled with sadness. The only song they had to sing was a sad one of despair.

We understand them, don't we? You and I have been there many times. Oftentimes, the only songs we feel like singing in life are songs in minor keys because life presents many experiences that are difficult for us to handle, and it seems as if evil and wrong reign. We are sick and pray for healing, but healing does not come. We want to right injustices and work to right them, but they are not changed. We begin to feel that it is useless to even try. Others always seem to get the breaks. Like Habakkuk, we wonder why the righteous suffer and the evil prosper. We don't always understand. We cannot make any sense out of heartbreaking tragedy and terrible violence. Sometimes all we seem to see in life is the triumph of evil and the triumph of wrong, and we have a tendency to believe that is all there is.

But the disciples learned that the resurrection followed the crucifixion and that changed their lives. They began to sing a new song. Wrong would be swallowed up by right, hopelessness would give way to joy, death would be conquered by life. They believed that the way of Christ was the right way, no matter what. At times, it didn't seem like it. Their little movement seemed about to be swept from the face of the earth, but they did not give up. They kept witnessing because they believed that what they were doing was right and would be victorious in the end.

At times all people see is the cross. However, the cross isn't the last fact in God's plan. A story from English history illustrates this point. Napoleon and Wellington were fighting at Waterloo. All England waited to hear the outcome. Signals flashed reports of the battle across the English Channel. On a foggy morning, the signal spelled out the words, "Wellington defeated." That's all the people on the English side of the channel saw. Despair and sorrow and sadness swept through the streets of London and all across England. Napoleon had won; there was no joy. But in the afternoon, the fog cleared away, and the signal came again: "Wellington defeated the enemy." They received the whole message, the right story. Immediately the people's mood changed from hopelessness to joy, from defeat to victory. They knew all the facts then, and they were victorious, not defeated.[2]

Sometimes the fogs of life's experiences cause us to see only our cross. However, Easter reminds us that there is resurrection. When all the facts are in, when all is said and done, goodness and righteousness and love and joy and Christ's way will reign supreme. Here is a verse we can sing loud and clear: "Goodness and righteousness, they will win, and we who live by them and seek them will know one day the joy of victory."

II. Death Is Not the End

The resurrection wrestles with one of the basic problems of life—the problem of death. We don't like to think about or talk about death. We hide death behind antiseptic hospital walls and in funeral parlors and in beautiful cemeteries. We don't want to face up to the fact of death. We don't want to think about the fact that every single one of us will one day die. That's a chilling note, and it sends chords of disharmony all through our spirits. We do not like to hear that tune. However, we never learn to live until we come face-to-face with what we think and do about the experience of death.

The disciples thought death was the end. The Jewish people, for the most part, did not believe in an afterlife as we do. Many did not believe in a resurrection. Death was the end. When Christ was crucified, that was it. There was no more! The end! Then the unbelievable happened! They saw it! Christ rose from the dead! He was alive! That made all the difference in their lives. Before that event, they had to run to hide in the darkness, afraid for their lives, afraid of death. After that experience, they went anywhere to tell the message of Christ and did not fear for their lives. Death was no longer an insurmountable barrier. Death was a barrier that could be passed through, overcome; and the reason they felt that way was because Christ had done it, and they saw it and believed.

If a man dies, shall he live again? We want to know. We are interested in the fact of life after death. Is there life after death? There has been some scientific investigation into that very fact, and some interesting results have occurred. One book deals with the experiences of several people across our country who have died on operating tables and in hospital beds but have been brought back to life. These people have shared the experiences and feelings they had when they were "dead."

Although they were separated by miles and miles and did not know each other, it's amazing how similar their experiences were. The conclusion of that study is this: There is life beyond death.[3]

Dr. Elisabeth Kübler-Ross is an expert in the field of death and dying. When she began her studies years ago with terminally ill patients, she held the conviction that there was "no life after death." But after years of dealing with people experiencing death, she has become convinced, beyond a shadow of a doubt to her, that there is more beyond.[4]

What the Bible has been saying for two thousand years is true, and we are just beginning to see it scientifically. Death is not the final note. There are more notes to be played. For us it means we can stand in the face of that which seems so final and say it is not so! We can stand in the presence of death and know that it, too, will pass. We have that hope.

Reuel Howe had a friend who had terminal cancer. Howe went to visit his friend one day, now knowing what to say. He was amazed to find the friend in control of himself. He told Howe:

When I began to work through this experience, I made an amazing discovery. And it is this: "For every exit, there is an entrance." All the way through my life I have been having to give up things in order to get things. I've had exits in order to get entrances. I had to give up something in order to go to school. I had to give up something in order to take a job. I had to give up single life in order to get married. All the way through my life, I've died a hundred deaths. I have had to die for something in order to get something new and better. For every exit, there is an entrance. And death is one more exit to that which is more.

He died, and Howe was asked to have the funeral. It was a difficult experience for him. The loss of that loved one hurt, and he was overcome by grief. As he was walking down the aisle in front of the casket, he noticed written on the back wall, courtesy of the fire marshall, the word that summed up the experience of his friend's life and the faith that he had. That one word was "EXIT."[5]

For every exit, there is an entrance. Death is an exit that leads to more. No exit! That's what the disciples said before the resurrection. After it, exits unlimited! This is the message of Easter. We can stand in the presence of death and sing, with faith and courage and hope, "More Beyond!"

III. Christ Is Alive Forever

Christ's death devastated the disciples, for they had trusted Him. They had invested their lives in Him. They had left jobs and families and security and safety. They thought it would be all right. He would be with them, and He would guide and protect them and take care of them. Now He was dead and gone. No wonder they were afraid, for they were so alone. They felt like no one was there to help them. No one could guide them. No one could protect them. They were left alone. So they ran.

Then the disciples heard the Easter song, "He is risen." They began to sing their new song: "You killed Him. You *thought* you could kill Him. You couldn't! He came back from the dead! He is alive! He is alive within our lives! He will be alive forevermore!" They knew it. They knew the joy of what it is to be in Christ. They knew His presence. They knew He was alive because He was alive within their lives.

This is the good news about Easter. Not only is there life beyond death but also there can be life before it. Each of us can experience the joy of living, abundant and rich and deep; and we can do that because Christ is alive now. He is alive, seeking to come and to minister to all of us. Nothing can keep Him from us: not sin, not death. He defeated all of that in the cross. He comes to say, "Look! I want to be with you. Nothing can keep me from it. I want to help you if you'll let me." Since He is alive and loose in the world, we can meet Him. We can discover through faith His presence in our lives, and it gives us joy and strength and hope for living.

We need Christ's presence to sustain and encourage and give hope. I read the story of parents who returned from the cemetery after burying their fourteen-year-old son to discover that another of their children had died with diphtheria. They were left with one three-year-old child. The second funeral service was held on Easter. They tried to make it a worshipful experience. The church was crowded. The congregation sang a triumphant hymn. But the father was numbed by his losses and could not utter a word. Then, as was customary in that church, the worshipers began to recite the Apostles' Creed, an affirmation of their belief: "I believe in God the Father Almighty, Maker of heaven and earth: And in Jesus Christ his only Son our Lord: . . . I believe in the Holy Ghost: . . . The Resurrection of the body." As the father said those words, he was reminded of the source of his roots, of his health, and of his strength. He began to say them with courage and with affirmation. He sang the next song with hope and with faith. A little boy had been watching the grieving father. As the boy left the church he said to his own father, "They really believe that Easter thing, don't they?"

"What's that?" the father asked.

"They believe that big thing about Easter, about life."

"Yes, they do. Not only life beyond, but life now."[6]

We need to discover in our own experiences that Christ is here in the presence of the Holy Spirit to give us help when we need it, to give us love, and to give us forgiveness for our sins. Easter is that discovery. He is alive! Now!

The song of Easter is a song that ought to be sung with trumpets and loud noises. Uncertain sounds do not belong in this song because it is a song that is right and pure. The first verse of it says that right and goodness are the victors, that wrong and evil fail. We ought to sing that every day, loudly and clearly. The second verse tells us that death is not the end, that there is more beyond. The last verse says that Christ is alive, now and forevermore! We ought to sing that, for it is the hope of our salvation.

Those are the verses, but there is one more thing. Here is the chorus: "He lives, and because He lives, so can we!" For this is the Easter message. It comes to us personally, and it comes to us saying that every one of us can know the joy of Christ. This is how we know that the resurrection is true. You and I know He lives because we have experienced the truth of the Bible in some place, somewhere, sometimes. We have experienced His presence in our lives. We know He lives because He lives within our hearts. The chorus we can all sing is that we know *Him!* We have a song to sing no matter how dark the darkness or how difficult the road. When we think about the fact that Christ lives and lives forever, we can sing only one kind of song. It's a "hallelujah chorus!" It's an "amen." It's a "praise God!" I hope that every one of us will sing it. Not just today, but every day we live until death, and beyond it!

Notes

1. John Redhead, "God's Singing Tower," Presbyterian Series of *The Protestant Hour,* 26 Feb.-2 Apr. 1967, p. 1.

2. Ibid, p. 2.

3. Raymond Massey, *Life After Life* (New York, Banton Books, 1975).

4. Elisabeth Kübler-Ross, *On Death and Dying* (New York: MacMillan, 1969).

5. John Claypool, "The Saga of Life: Senior Adulthood," Sermon: Broadway Baptist Church, Fort Worth, Tex., 28 Sept. 1976, pp. 6-7.

6. Charles Trentham, *Getting on Top of Your Troubles* (Nashville: Broadman Press, 1966), pp. 100-101.

14

The Resurrection: The Great Affirmation

Mark 16:1-8

"The third day he rose again from the dead." In those few brief words, the apostles told about the event of the resurrection, almost as if it were a matter-of-fact happening. But if that event had not occurred, they would have had nothing to write about, no hope to proclaim. The foundation stone of the disciples' faith and the foundation stone of our faith centers around that statement: "The third day he rose again from the dead."

People ask me what is the most important doctrine of our faith. It's easy to answer. He rose from the dead! If Christ had not risen from the dead, we would have hardly heard of Him. He would have been just another good man who lived a good life for good causes, but who died a martyr's death, and that was that. A memory, a footnote in history, but that is all. Since the cry rang throughout history that He rose from the dead, we know of Him. There was no one like Him before. There has not been anyone like Him since. He is unique. He rose from the dead!

I can't prove the resurrection beyond a shadow of an intellectual doubt. People would like for me to do it, but I can't. All I can do is to present evidence that seems to support it. We can talk about the fact that the early Christians who were all Jews changed their day of worship from the sabbath to Sunday. It would have taken something very drastic to cause them to change that tradition; the resurrection was that drastic. They began to worship on Sunday because they believed Christ rose from the dead on that day. We can talk about the fact that the church has survived for 2,000 years. Monuments to dead persons usually don't; but the church has survived because it's not a museum for Christ, but it is a place of His presence. Christ has kept the church alive and going strong. We can talk about the disciples, who were cowards before the resurrection; after the resurrection, they were courageous disciples willing to throw their lives away for Christ's sake. They believed He was alive. Some people have accused the disciples of stealing the body of Jesus from the tomb. That's a ridiculous idea. I do not think that the disciples would willingly have allowed themselves to be crucified on crosses and to die for what they knew was a lie. Some people have said that the religious leaders stole the body of Jesus, but all they had to do anytime to refute the disciples' claim and put a stop to the Christian movement was to produce Jesus' body. They couldn't produce it because they didn't have it. We can talk about the pros and cons, but one can't prove the resurrection that way. The resurrection has to be trusted. It is a matter of faith. We trust Christ and who He is and what He's done. In the trusting is the discovery. We know Christ is alive because we have experienced Him ourselves. We do that through faith. There's no other way to come to Christ except through faith.

Why is the resurrection the great affirmation for us? Why do we herald it so much and celebrate it so joyously? The resurrection affirms everything Jesus was and everything Jesus is.

I. Jesus Is the Son of God

Jesus tried to teach the disciples that He was the Messiah, the One sent from God. All of Jesus' healings were attempts to show the power of God that was available in Him and through Him. He had told the people over and over again that the kingdom of God had already begun in Him and that all they had to do to be part of the kingdom was to trust Him. They didn't understand. Even the disciples didn't understand. They ran before the crucifixion. After the crucifixion, their future was settled. Christ was dead. Their hopes had been misplaced. He wasn't who they thought He was. They had hoped that He might be the Messiah; but how could He be, dead in that tomb?

After the resurrection, the disciples believed! After the resurrection, they were willing to go anywhere to serve Him. They believed that He was who He said He was. Only God could have the power to overcome death. Only God could do what He had done in Christ. They became serious about everything He said and serious about everything He had done. They began to preach it and to teach it, convinced beyond a shadow of a doubt that Jesus was God with them.

That's what our doctrine of the incarnation is about. It means "God in flesh and bones"; Jesus was God with us. We can't prove that beyond a shadow of a doubt either, but the resurrection makes it easier to believe. The resurrection gives us the assurance that Christ God with us. The testimony of all of the disciples was that Christ was God Himself. The resurrection proves Jesus was who He said He was. All that He did, all that He taught, was seconded. The resurrection proved He was right.

The picture "Easter Eve" by Eugene Burnand shows all the disciples on Easter eve. They are in the upper room where they had celebrated the Lord's Supper. How sorrowful they are. Thomas sits with his chin in his hand, looking out into nothing, for nothing seems to have hope. Peter sits with his head bowed. He had denied Jesus, and he feels ashamed, so hopeless. John had been at the crucifixion and is overcome by sorrow. There is nothing to do but to weep. But another picture shows Easter Day and how the disciples had changed. Thomas is crying out, "My Lord and my God!" Peter is preaching about Christ, the Son of the living God. Everything had been changed because of one event. Christ rose, and the message the disciples went out to tell everybody was that He is God with us. Alive forever![1]

At times, we may wonder; at times, we may doubt it. However, the resurrection is the word that we have that God has come to be with us. In all experiences of life, He is still with us because He is alive in the presence of His Spirit.

II. Jesus Has the Power to Save Us

Jesus told the disciples that He had come to save them from their sins. They needed salvation. They had become slaves to the power of evil. Jesus offered salvation: "I'll break the power of sin in your life. I'll give you new life. I'll give you joy. Sin is keeping you from loving others. I'll teach you to love one another. I can do these things for you if you trust me."

The disciples began to believe in Jesus. Then the cross. How could Christ do anything for them? Someone who could come under the power of sin and be conquered by it was no savior for them. A dead Jesus could do them no good.

Then the disciples heard the women's shouts, "He is alive!" Sin had done everything it could do to Him, but it could not keep Him in the grave. They began to understand. Christ did have the power over sin. Christ did have the ability to help break the bondage that they had found themselves in.

That's a resurrection message for every one of us. Since Christ rose from the dead, sin cannot conquer Him. He knows what we need. He knows how to forgive us. He knows how to help us overcome our sins.

He is able to deliver us. He is not the Christ who lived and died. He is the *living* Christ who died and rose again to forgive us of our sins. He has the power to save us.

Some years ago in England, Charles Bradlaugh used to go around debunking the Christian religion. He claimed Christianity was all a bunch of nothing. One day, he challenged Hugh Price Hughes, a pastor of one of the missions in town, to debate the merits of Christian faith against his idea that the Christian faith was worthless. Hughes agreed, and they set the time and the place. Hughes said:

> I am going to bring to that meeting one hundred people who have been touched by the love and power of Christ. They will be people from poverty-stricken areas, people who have been caught in all kinds of sin and habits, but they have been touched by the power of God and have overcome it. They will come and testify to the power of Christ in their lives and what He has done for them. What I ask you to do is to bring one hundred people who will testify to what good your gospel of infidelity has done.

The night came for the debate, and the crowd came to hear it. The hundred people marched in with Hughes, people from all walks of life, most of them had known hard times. They were ready to give their testimonies to the fact that Christ had delivered them. They waited for Bradlaugh and his people, but they didn't show up.[2]

That's not surprising. How can one argue with a life that's been changed by Jesus Christ? One just can't. The one unanswerable argument for the resurrection is a life that has known the power of the risen Christ. Christ is able to change us, to make us new, to deliver us from all of the sins in which we are caught. He has the power, and He's available even now to do it for us. Trusting Christ means turning our lives over to His love. It means letting Him have control of us. He can do it. He is alive and able.

III. Christ's Way Will Be Triumphant

Christ told the disciples, "Be of good cheer, I have overcome the world" (John 16:33). That means Christ's ways are going to triumph. Love will conquer hate. Good will conquer evil. Satan will be defeated by Christ. Even death will be overcome by life.

But on that Friday when Jesus was nailed to the cross, it looked as if everything bad had won. Evil had conquered; death had certainly conquered Christ. It seemed that Satan had thrown his best at Jesus and had won the victory. That Good Friday was dark Friday in human history. Nothing good happened there.

In despair, the disciples fled. There were no songs of joy, only tears of sorrow. But then, Easter! Out of the darkness came the disciples to sing. The tears of sorrow were swallowed up in tears of joy. Now they knew. Nothing could defeat Jesus Christ! He rose from the dead! He lives again!

The resurrection tells us that love will triumph, that life will triumph. Christ will triumph. Whatever seems to be your enemy, eventually it will fall at the feet of Jesus Christ. Buddha died, Mohammed died, Confucius died, Joseph Smith died, and Karl Marx died. Jesus Christ died, *but* He rose from the dead! No one else has done that! No one else can do it! Jesus Christ is the One!

The heart of our faith is the affirmation that only one kingdom lives forever, God's kingdom. In 1799, Napoleon's forces were going through Austria, and 18,000 French troops camped on the hills outside the village of Feldkirch. They were ready to conquer the city the next day. People in the city had a meeting and decided the next morning to go out and offer to the general the keys to their city and plead for mercy. They could not defeat the enemy at their doorstep. The next morning was Easter. As the custom was, at dawn the church bells began to ring, calling the people to worship to celebrate the magnificent event of the resurrection. All the church bells were pealing that joyful sound, and the general heard it. The only conclusion he could come to was that during the night, the Austrian army must have slipped into the city. Therefore, he gathered his 18,000 troops and turned and went away, feeling he could not conquer the city.[3]

In a way, the bells of Easter ring out loudly and clearly to tell us that all the enemies that camp around us, threatening as they are, will fall back when the bells of Easter ring. They know they cannot win. This is the Easter message. This is what the resurrection affirms: Jesus Christ will accomplish what He set out to do. What He set out to do was to establish an eternal kingdom that will be forever.

What is the foundation of our faith? Jesus rose from the dead! That is the hope of our faith. One of my favorite stories of Easter has to do with a boy named Philip. He was a down's syndrome child. His family took him to church regularly. The Sunday after Easter, the third grade Sunday School teacher had a very good idea. He gave an empty plastic egg to each boy and said, "I want you to go outside on this beautiful day and find something that symbolizes to you Easter and the new life that Christ has brought." The boys went outside to collect items to put in their eggs. Back in the classroom the eggs were opened. A beautiful flower was in one egg, and everyone was happy about that. Another one was opened and there was a butterfly in it, a symbol of new life. They opened another, and there was a rock. Somebody said, "What does that have to do with new life at Easter?" The boy said, "I thought you'd say that. I knew you would be getting flowers and pretty things, but I wanted to be different. So I got a rock because a rock is different, and that's what new life and Easter means to me. I can be different. I am different. I am unique." The teacher thought to himself, *What a profound thought from an eight-year-old boy.* Then they opened another egg, and it was empty. They began to complain; somebody didn't play by the rules. Somebody cheated. Philip tugged at his teacher. They said, "Philip, you dummy. You didn't play the game right. Can't you ever learn?" Philip said, "I did. That's what Easter means. Don't you see? The tomb is empty."[4]

Somehow, Philip became part of the group. He was right! The tomb is empty. That means Christ is alive. Christ is right where we are, always!

Notes

1. John W. Rilling, "The Trumpets of Triumph," *The Clergy Journal,* Mar. 1977, pp. 3-4.

2. Ralph Ward, Jr., "Witnesses of the Resurrection," *Pulpit Digest,* Mar. 1956, p. 62.

3. Frank Norfleet, *Survey,* Aug. 1963, p. 21.

4. Craig Biddle III, "The Empty Tomb," *Master Sermons,* Apr. 1980, pp. 178-180.

15

Easter Discoveries

John 20:1-23

Something happened on that Easter morning nearly 2,000 years ago which changed the destiny of humanity. The Scriptures tell that Jesus rose from the dead! They say it as a matter of fact, as if everybody was supposed to know it. Those who wrote the Scriptures surely did. The resurrection had been a life-changing event for them. Before the resurrection, they were cringing cowards, fleeing for their lives. After the resurrection, they became courageous challengers of the world, running into swords and coliseums and into death, willing to give their lives for the One they called the risen Christ. They believed He was alive.

Is it true? That's what the world wants to know. People want to believe it, but it seems unbelievable. Prove it to us. Give us some facts to help us know for sure. No amount of evidence we can marshall will ever be enough to prove the resurrection. It cannot be done. It is a matter of faith. That moment we trust Christ as our Savior and follow Him, we discover that it *is* true. He lives within us! He is alive! Easter is not a time to argue for the resurrection. Easter is a time to underline what it means because it *is* true.

What does the resurrection mean for us today? In the midst of a world torn by war and poverty and sickness and hate, in the midst of lives faced with cancer and leukemia and divorce and discouragement and unemployment, what does the resurrection have to say? What did the disciples discover, and what can be discovered anew this Easter?

I. Service to Christ Has Meaning

Between that Friday and Sunday, the disciples fled. They fled because they were confused, discouraged, fearful. They had trusted Jesus, they had believed that He was going to bring in the kingdom. For three years, they had followed Him at great personal sacrifice. They had left home, families, and jobs behind, and now they were beginning to wonder why.

All the words He taught them seemed to be useless. All the people He had helped, He only helped them live lives of no hope. All that they did for Him seemed like a waste of time.

Have you ever felt like that? As you have tried to do your part for Christ, have you ever had moments when you wondered if it were worth it at all? I talked to a Sunday School teacher who had tried to help a boy in his class, a young teenager. The teacher had stayed with the boy and had done things with him and had loved the boy, but he got into the wrong crowd and got into trouble with the law and with drugs. Today he is behind bars. The man said, "It was just no use. I did everything I could, but it was just no use. It doesn't do any good, it is just a waste of time."

It can seem that way. Preachers preach sermons hoping people will change and find Christ, but many never do. Believers speak up for Christ in discussion groups at school or at work, but few take them seriously. Believers try to live good, Christian lives, but no one seems to care. Believers are involved in the ministries of the church, but nothing positive seems to happen.

I suspect that most of us have lived between the cross and the empty tomb and known the discouragement and the frustration of it. But Easter dawned, and when it came to the disciples, it brought to them an awareness that all that they had done, what they had taught and learned, all the people they had helped, was not in vain. The kingdom of God was going to come, and nothing was going to stop it. All service rendered to Christ was worthwhile. So they went about planting flowers, flowers that they might not see bloom, but they were confident that as they planted the seed, that somewhere, sometime, someplace, bloom they would!

That's what Easter tells those of us who get discouraged and frustrated. It tells us to keep on going. Don't quit! It is worthwhile! Do the good works, live the good life, speak the good words. Someplace, somewhere, sometime a word will strike home, a deed will matter, the life will be noticed. This is the way it works. No work, no word is wasted!

A man told a minister friend, "Why don't you give up on all this Jesus stuff? It's no good. You've been preaching at it for thirty-some years and take a look at the world. It still struggles with war, is still troubled with hate and immorality. It's not going to get any better. All your words and all your deeds don't do any good. Why don't you go ahead and admit it?" The preacher said, "I'm not ready to do that yet. Let's just wait a little bit longer, and then we'll see!"

How long do we wait? Why not to the end, and let's see then? Easter tells us that when the end comes God's kingdom and all that has been done for it will live forever.

II. Help Is Available in Life

The disciples felt abandoned when Christ died. He had helped them in the past. Who would help them now? Life had been hard for them before, now it could only get harder. They were helpless. Then the Easter dawned and the message went out through the land. He is alive! He has risen! Before long, they discovered it was true. Jesus appeared to them and said that His presence would be with them still, to guide them, to strengthen them, and to help them. So they went into the world to face whippings and beatings and all kinds of suffering. They went to face death triumphantly, courageously, because they believed that the power of the risen Christ would be with them. And He was! He did not fail them. They were not alone.

We must learn to live in the presence of Christ. Hopefully, we already have. In the midst of life, there is a power to help us. Christ is alive and comes to help us face our struggles, not bypass them, not to take them away, but to give us the strength to deal with them, and to face them courageously. In the midst of disappointment, He comes to give us strength to get up and at it again. In the midst of sickness, He comes to give us the courage to deal with it. In the midst of loneliness, He comes to be our friend. In the midst of fear, He comes to give us a faith that frightens fear away. In the midst of guilt, He comes to bring us forgiveness. Whatever need you have, Christ can meet it. This is what Easter tells us. No darkness is so dark that the light of Christ cannot shine in it. We have no needs that Christ cannot help us face.

A boy had been crippled for some time. His father took him to a church that had been known for miracles of healing. The boy entered the church, believing that his legs would be healed and he could throw his crutches away. Kneeling, Father and son prayed earnestly for healing. As the boy prayed, he felt strangely within himself that there was a power and a presence with him. When they finished praying and walked out of the church, the boy had to do so with his crutches. The boy's legs had not been healed physically, but he had been healed. In that experience, he had discovered the presence of Christ, the power of Christ that would help him live in this life, even with his crutches. His father said, "I'm sorry that your prayer wasn't answered." The boy said, "But it was answered. I have been healed."[1]

Whatever struggles we face, whatever difficulties we bear, we do not have to bear them alone. The living Christ helps us.

III. Death Is Not the End

The disciples were like us. They did not believe that when a person was dead, he rose again. When Christ was crucified, that was it. There was no more to be said, all was lost. When they heard the truth that He was alive, they couldn't believe it. They had a hard time understanding it. Thomas said, "Unless I see . . . I will not believe" (John 20:25). But finally, they did see. They did believe, and they went out to the world with this one truth: Christ has conquered death. No longer did they fear death. Instead, they laughed at it and faced it with courage because they believed that it had been conquered.

Is there life after death? The resurrection message shouts out loud and clear: *yes!* We have trouble believing it still. We want somebody to prove it to us. We're very interested in anything that will prove there is life after death. There's a great deal of interest in books like *Life After Death*[2] where people supposedly died and had wonderful experiences and came back to tell about them. The stories are interesting stories to read, but I have some problems with that evidence. Did the people really die, or were they merely in the process of dying? None had been dead for *three* days and come back. Were they really dead? That is a question unanswered. Believers and nonbelievers had similar experiences; their attitude of faith made no difference. That seems to question what we have been taught to believe. While all of this evidence is interesting, it proves nothing. The resurrection rests upon faith in who Jesus Christ was, what He was, and what He did. Can we trust Him? Did He lie to us? Did He fail the disciples? Will He fail us? The resurrection is a matter for the believer, a matter of faith. When we put our faith in Jesus Christ, the resurrection becomes true for us and we discover that we participate in life that is eternal because Christ is eternal.

What will life after death be like? No one really knows. What happens to us in the moment of death? The analogy I like best has to do with birth. When we were in our mother's womb, we were very comfortable and warm. All of our needs were met. We were very content there. All of a sudden, we were being pushed out to another world, and we didn't know what it would be like. What would meet us? Who would greet us? Would our needs be met? Finally we were born, into a noisy world, to a world of light, a world of masked strangers. We discovered people waiting for us, waiting to tend to our every need, waiting to hold us close, waiting to love us. All of our needs were met. We were born into a world that was far greater than we'd had before.

I believe our death is a new birth. I don't know what lies beyond it, but I believe that there are those waiting for me, that my every need will be met. That world is far better than the one I now know. One fact I do believe: There will be one person to meet me. The Christ who has been sufficient for my needs here will be that same Christ who meets me there.

That will be enough, and I will be able to say, "O Death, where is thy victory?/O Death, where is thy sting?" (1 Cor. 15:55). Gone, swallowed up in victory through Christ Jesus, our Lord! Death is not the final door for us, but just one more door that leads to more life.

The disciples discovered in Easter that their faith in Christ was not misplaced. He could be trusted. From that moment on, everything they did had meaning because it would last. Every darkness they lived through, they lived through because they knew in the midst of it was the light of Christ. Even when they had to face death, and all of them did, they did so with courage because they believed it was not the end, but a new beginning.

Every year thousands of people climb a mountain in the Italian Alps, passing the "stations of the cross" to stand at an outdoor crucifix. One tourist noticed a little trail that led beyond the cross. He fought through the rough thicket and, to his surprise, came upon another shrine, a shrine that symbolized the empty tomb. It was neglected. The brush had grown up around it. Almost everyone had gotten as far as the cross, but there they stopped.[3]

Far too many have gotten to the cross and known the despair and the heartbreak and the unhappiness and the difficulty of this world and have not passed the cross to the empty tomb. They have not discovered that life is possible because Christ is alive.

We can bypass all that would defeat us, we can conquer all that would destroy us, by going past the cross to the empty tomb to the living Christ, One we can know. We know Him through faith. We know Him by trusting Him, by saying that now and forevermore we will follow Him, love Him, and let Him be our Savior and Lord. When we make that commitment and live it, we will discover that Easter is every day.

Notes

1. C. W. Kirkpatrick, "Mountains That Cannot be Moved," *The Pulpit,* Jan. 1955, p. 20.

2. Raymond Moody, *Life After Death* (New York: Bantan Books, 1975).

3. Lavonn Brown, "The Other Half of the Rainbow," *Sermons and Services for Special Days,* ed. Jack Gulledge (Nashville: Convention Press, 1979), p. 21.